Chile: A Historical Interpretation

Crosscurrents in Latin America
Edited by Joseph S. Tulchin

CHILE:
A HISTORICAL INTERPRETATION

JAY KINSBRUNER

Harper & Row, Publishers
New York, Evanston, San Francisco, London

Maps by Willow Roberts.

CHILE: A HISTORICAL INTERPRETATION

LIBRARY OF CONGRESS CATALOG CARD NUMBER: 73-5674

STANDARD BOOK NUMBER: 06-136131-3
Designed by Ann Scrimgeour

For Karen

CONTENTS

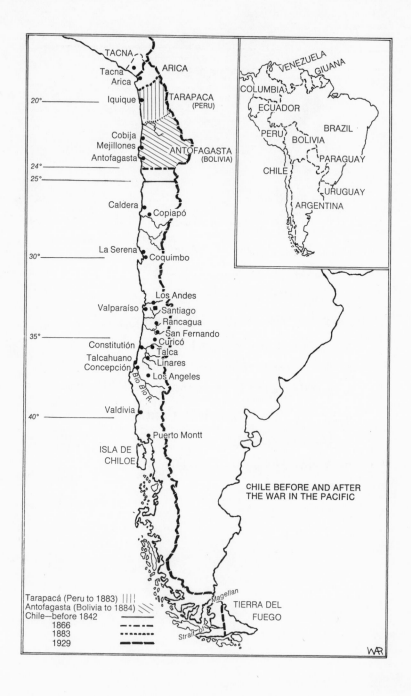

TACNA
Tacna
Arica
ARICA

20° Iquique
TARAPACA
(PERU)

Cobija
Mejillones
Antofagasta
ANTOFAGASTA
(BOLIVIA)

24°
25°

Caldera
Copiapó

La Serena
30° Coquimbo

Los Andes
Valparaíso Santiago
Rancagua
San Fernando
35° Curicó
Constitución Talca
Talcahuano Linares
Concepción Los Angeles

Bio Bio R.

40° Valdivia

Puerto Montt

ISLA DE
CHILOE

VENEZUELA
GIUANA
COLUMBIA
ECUADOR
PERU BRAZIL
BOLIVIA
PARAGUAY
CHILE
URUGUAY
ARGENTINA

CHILE BEFORE AND AFTER
THE WAR IN THE PACIFIC

Magellan
TIERRA DEL
FUEGO

Strait of

Tarapacá (Peru to 1883) ||||
Antofagasta (Bolivia to 1884)
Chile—before 1842
1866
1883
1929

WAR

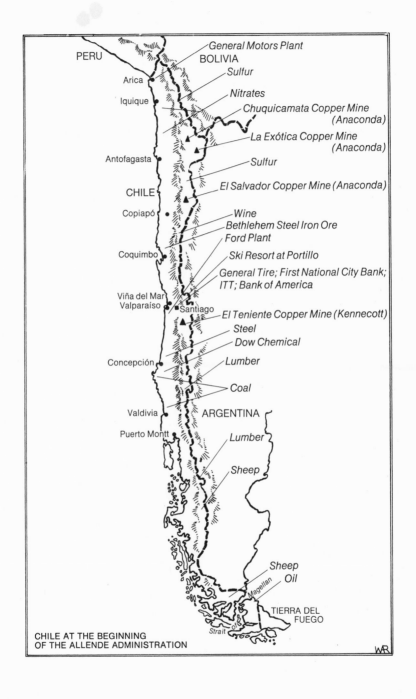

CHILE AT THE BEGINNING
OF THE ALLENDE ADMINISTRATION

INTRODUCTION

Rather than a history of Chile, this book is an interpretation of that history. It is an attempt to range through several centuries of an anguished nation's past in an effort to make current events a bit more understandable and hopefully to stimulate further thought and investigation. While I should be pleased if other historians find my interpretation significant, the book is intended especially for students, including those in survey courses who usually are not able to spend all or most of a term on one country. I have not tried to answer all the questions that might arise from a discussion of more than four centuries of history; in fact, if the book is successful as an interpretation, it will raise new questions. But I have tried to provide a perspective around which students may make sense of Chilean history as they read it in this book and elsewhere, a perspective which will enable the student to arrive at his own answers to the problems I have dealt with, the questions I have raised, and, perhaps most importantly, the issues I have not discussed.

Since it is an interpretation, it must be selective in its use of historical material. Not all events or aspects of Chilean history will be mentioned; only those will be dealt with that are pertinent to the basic themes developed in the narrative. Briefly, some of these themes are (1) that Chile was never controlled exclusively by a landed aristocracy, (2) that the Chilean economy has always been centrally capitalist rather than feudal, (3) that even with one of the world's most extravagant topographies and its seeming isolation, Chile has always been directly in the mainstream of Western development, and finally (4) that neocolonialism was never the only consequential factor in Chilean evolution. (Even in the twentieth century it has been one of several significant factors.)

These themes were not arrived at casually. They represent my position on critical historiographical issues that are pertinent for an understanding of present-day Chile. For instance, so many Chileans believe that the determining factor in their country's evolution since independence has been neocolonialism and that their country's experience with international capitalism has traditionally been a dismal failure that they are inclined to lose sight of the fact that the country's evolution was determined by many factors and that nineteenth-century governments were spirited and bold in their treatment of foreigners and foreign nations. This belief has contributed to a persuasive pessimism that has had serious political consequences. Chile's strident "anti-imperialism" reflects not only current social, economic, and political needs, but an emotional reaction to a seemingly long history of grievous neocolonialism. The extent of the emotional reaction is not always justified by the historical record.

Chile is at a crossroads in its history. Socialist Salvador Allende was elected president in 1970 on the promise to socialize the Chilean system through constitutional means. At this writing it is evident that it is not an easy task he has set for himself; and, so far from bringing about socialism through constitutional means, he may not be able to preside over a stable economy much less effect a permanent revision of the traditional system through constitutional means. If Allende goes further to the left (as it is, Socialists in Chile are more radical than Communists), as he might well do in order to mollify the extreme left in his *Unidad Popular* coalition, the middle and lower middle classes are likely to be the first to suffer. Many members of these two classes still function on the basis of the profit motive and private ownership of property. The upper class already knows where it stands with Allende; now the broad middle class is finding out where it stands. Without the middle class—with its upper and lower fringes—it is doubtful that Chile could have either its traditional liberal democracy or its modified capitalism.

Several terms used in this book require special clarification. The first is "active citizenry," a term frequently used by Chileans in their constitutions. In the early national period (the post-1810 period) *ciudadanos activos* referred to those Chileans who were permitted to vote. There were then enough restrictions on the franchise to keep the active citizenry fairly small. For many decades the active citizenry ran Chile. Later in the nineteenth century franchise requirements were reduced, but as it turned out the newly enfranchised possessed the vote but not power. There were many ways for government officials and laymen alike to control votes—bribes, fraud, physical intimidation, job intimidation, and so on. In the early nineteenth century when fewer people voted, governments were fairly representative of the enfranchised population. This would not be so again until well into the twentieth century.

I have used the terms "feudalism" and "capitalism" without defining them systematically, because there are several accepted definitions of each term. A satisfactory discussion of the two terms would require a lengthy chapter or two. Definitions of feudalism—some quite antithetical to others—range from the political to the economic and social. In my use of the term "feudalism" I have steered a middle road among the three categories, stressing labor service requirements for land usage as a remnant of feudalism in the modern period.

There are three widely accepted definitions of capitalism. One emphasizes production for distant markets; another (probably the one most North Americans accept), an economic system in which profit motive, private initiative, and a free market system reign supreme. The third, Marx's definition, is probably the most popular in the world at large. For Marx, capitalism is the stage in the development of commodity production at which point labor itself becomes a commodity and is bought and sold as any other commodity. When this stage of economic development is reached, the means of production are owned by one class of society, one that represents a minority of the population, and the labor on which the means of production depends is owned by the other class of society, the propertyless class which has only its labor to sell. The first two definitions can pertain to any era of history. According to them capitalism has always existed in some place or other throughout most of history. Marx's definition, however, pertains only to the modern era. It is the only one that deals specifically with the social problems attendant upon the transition from pre-industrial to industrial economies, and as such it is the most helpful for an understanding of contemporary Latin America.[1]

Examining Chile's colonial history according to each of the three definitions leads one to believe that its economy was basically capitalist and not feudal, although it had prominent feudal holdovers. By the time we get to the late colonial period and the early nineteenth century, the first two definitions become less useful than the third. When discussing Chilean capitalism from about the eighteenth century, I have in mind especially Marx's definition. Chile certainly had a fundamentally capitalist economy at the time of its independence, but it was less mature than many of its competitors in the world capitalist system. This left the new country severely disadvantaged.

This book represents a ten-year academic interest in Chilean history. During this time I have become indebted to many people. I should like to thank first the Fulbright Commission for an Inter-American Cultural Grant that got me to Chile in 1963. Grants and fellowships from the Organization of American States, the Social Science Research Council, and the American Philosophical Society allowed me to carry out research there during the summers of 1965, 1967, and 1969, respectively. A Fulbright lectureship to Venezuela for the fall of 1967 afforded me the opportunity of making firsthand comparisons with Chile and seeing its recent development from a somewhat different perspective. I deeply appreciate the financial support of all these organizations.

I am tempted to mention the historians and archivists who have gone out of their way to help me in Chile and the United States since I first started studying Chilean history, but such a list simply would be too long. I trust they know how grateful I am. I am pleased to acknowledge, however, the efforts of several colleagues

[1] For an excellent discussion of the various definitions of capitalism see Maurice Dobb, *Studies in the Development of Capitalism,* rev. ed. (New York, 1968), pp. 1–32.

who read, criticized, and improved the manuscript for this book. Professor Ralph della Cava, Professor Arnold J. Bauer, Professor Marvin D. Bernstein, and Professor Joseph S. Tulchin read all or parts of it. Professor John E. Fagg guided the research and writing of my doctoral dissertation, from which the Wheelwright sections are taken. I thank them all. Any errors in fact or judgment remain my own responsibility.

In a brief interpretation no debt is greater than to the other scholars whose works one uses in formulating and supporting one's own positions. I have intended the bibliography to convey my appreciation to these scholars.

Many people connected with the Paul Klapper Library of Queens College helped me beyond the point of mere professional courtesy. Much of my work over the years would have been delayed considerably were it not for their efforts. I am especially indebted to Professor Solena V. Bryant and Leonard Cohen (now of the State University College at Cortland, New York).

Finally, I should like to thank my wife, Karen, not only for helping me through the traumatic moments often created by the various production deadlines, but for proofreading and editing the manuscript, galleys, and page proofs, always more than once and always apparently less harried than I knew her to be or than I was.

PART I
THE COLONIAL PERIOD

1
THE ESTABLISHMENT OF THE COLONY

The Spanish conquest and colonization of America was essentially an economic venture. Religious idealism and militarism were part of it and so too was a conspicuous interest in territorial aggrandizement, but at bottom the Spanish Crown sought financial wealth through empire. The opportunity to convert vast numbers of heathens, to flex the muscles of a military machine that had just defeated the Moors and ended the centuries-old reconquest of the Iberian Peninsula (and thus also to keep its soldiers occupied), and the opportunity to acquire territory for its own sake all had their attractions, but they were collateral benefits of the central quest for precious metals, raw materials, and captive markets.

By 1535, when the first Spanish expedition set out from Peru to explore Chile, the Spanish Crown had been authorizing colonization efforts in the New World for over forty years. More than just the first returns were in by then, and Crown, conquistador, and colonizer alike had been treated to the spectacle of imposing indigenous cultures, alluring wealth in the form of precious metals, and what appeared to be an unlimited labor supply. The impressive amounts of gold and silver taken from the Incas by Pizarro in the early 1530s further fired the zeal of his companions and rendered an expedition to the southern part of the continent unavoidable.

The splendors of Mexico and Peru did little to prepare the Spaniards for the relative poverty and, indeed, the native intransigence they would encounter in Chile. At the time of the conquest Chile was most densely populated in the south, from the Bío-Bío River down to the Maullín. Farther south in the Patagonian and archipelagic regions there were few inhabitants. North of the Bío-Bío the number of inhabitants thinned as one entered the arid desert. By the mid-1530s there were hundreds of thousands of Indians in Chile, perhaps even a million or more. But they did not form part of a highly advanced culture such as those the Spaniards had found in the lands of the Aztecs and Incas, nor was there a similarly advanced societal organization that could promise an easy and plentiful supply of labor.

The natives of Chile were divided into a limitless number of tribes and several racial and cultural groups. For the later history of Chile the most important were the Araucanians, as the Indians living south of the Bío-Bío were called by the Spaniards.[1] Except in time of war the highest social organization among the Araucanians was the tribe. In ordinary times tribes were merely mutual associations of families without a chief. In the event of war the tribe elected a chief, and when the seriousness of the situation suggested it, the tribe federated with other tribes. The larger group in turn elected a chief to prosecute the war effort. It is difficult to imagine a societal organization of tribes less nation-like and further removed from the complicated and sophisticated structures created by the Aztecs and Incas. Yet the Araucanians were bolder and more determined warriors than either the Aztecs or Incas, and, in fact, they were not defeated finally in battle until more than three centuries after the domination of the two northern cultures.

The first successful Spanish expedition to Chile was a modest venture, undertaken by Pedro de Valdivia, the highest ranking officer in Francisco Pizarro's army in Peru. Valdivia had acquired wealth in Peru, including an *encomienda*—a grant of Indian labor—and a silver mine. It was his idea to lead an expedition to Chile, a quite astonishing suggestion considering Chile's poor reputation among the Spaniards in Peru since the failure of a previous expedition led by Diego de Almagro. Yet in 1539 Pizarro granted Valdivia the necessary permission and elevated him to the rank of lieutenant governor for Chile.

Valdivia was an especially distinguished officer, but his personal fortune was not sufficient to bring together a very large expedition.

---

[1] Today most Chilean Indians live in the south, and although technically they are not all Mapuches, they are often referred to as such.

While some Spaniards might follow him through allegiance, many more would not risk their lives and time on an expedition to a place that had fallen into such disrepute as Chile. Valdivia could put together a force of only about 150 soldiers. He started on his expedition from Cuzco in January 1540 with little more than a dozen men. The others were to meet him en route.

After seven months of marching the enlarged expedition arrived at Copiapó, at the southern edge of the Atacama Desert. With them the Spaniards had several thousand Indian porters, *yanaconas,* including women and children. There was even a Spanish woman, Inés Suárez, one of the most famous of the conquest of Spanish America, who traveled with Valdivia. The conquistadors also brought with them domestic animals, European grains, and agricultural tools. Valdivia was determined to lead an expedition to colonize as well as conquer. In early 1541 the Spaniards reached the valley of the Mapocho River and established camp at the foot of a commanding hill they called Santa Lucía. On February 12, 1541, the town of Santiago was founded there.

Like leaders of expeditions before him in other parts of the New World, Valdivia was quick to institutionalize his position. Within weeks after the founding of Santiago, a *cabildo,* a town council, was established. This corporate body had a long heritage in medieval Spain and was the heart of Spanish urbanism, a potent force in the creation of the national monarchy. The cabildo of Santiago at first had two *alcaldes,* judges rather than mayors, although they had some administrative duties; six *regidores,* councilmen; a *procurador,* a town attorney; and a secretary. Valdivia himself appointed the members of the first cabildo. They in turn insisted that their leader and benefactor declare himself governor of Chile in the name of the king, rather than remain Pizarro's lieutenant governor. To lend respectability to this serious step, a *cabildo abierto,* an open cabildo, was convened, comprising traditionally the leading local citizens. There would be other cabildos abiertos during the colonial period with the one of September 18, 1810, taking the first step toward independence.

Valdivia now had his formal title and legal power, and Chile had a government in the cabildo of Santiago. A political structure, however simple, would have been meaningless in a colony without a visible means of self-support. Valdivia set out at once to establish a viable economic basis for his colony. Indian laborers were put to work in gold washings; others were conscripted for the construction of a ship for communication with Peru. But the Chilean Indians were not quite so submissive as the Spaniards expected or the colony required. Before much work could be accomplished there was a mass uprising by the Indians of the Aconcagua valley. The soldiers who guarded the Indian laborers at the gold washings and at the ship construction site were killed. In September 1541 Santiago itself was attacked and destroyed. The town was quickly rebuilt, but for the next two years, until supplies arrived from Peru, the Spaniards were confined more or less to Santiago and its environs.

Replenished by Peruvian supplies at the end of 1543, Valdivia once again undertook the expansion of his colony. To secure the road to Peru he ordered the founding of the northern town of La Serena. He himself undertook an expedition to the south and got to the region of the Bío-Bío, but there he was attacked by the fierce southern Indians who presented such a unique problem to the conquest and colonization of the New World. To deal with them Valdivia sent for additional troops and supplies. Civil war in Peru delayed their arrival, so Valdivia decided to go to Peru himself in 1547. Upon his arrival Valdivia supported the royal emissary against the Pizarro family and actually led the battle that decided the war in favor of the Crown's representative, who was now indebted to the Chilean governor.

Valdivia, therefore, had little trouble in securing supplies and additional troops. More than a hundred men were sent south, to be followed later by Valdivia with more men and supplies. Back in Chile Valdivia found La Serena destroyed by the Indians and ordered it rebuilt. And again he led an expedition to the south. The Araucanians he encountered on this trip were not less bold or violent than those met earlier, and their vigor suggested a means of colonization that had been tried and tested during the reconquest of the Iberian peninsula from the Moors and was already being employed in other parts of Spanish America: the use of towns, of urban centers to secure provincial and frontier regions. The conquest and colonization of Spanish America was, unlike that of North America, an urban rather than a rural effort. Towns, sometimes little more than forts, sometimes seemingly little more than rural agglomerations, were established and supported naturally here, by fiat there. To accomplish their tasks the towns were granted such authority over their local and at times provincial regions by the Crown that the more affluent ones could wield impressive power, at times presenting themselves as prominent and antagonistic forces to central colonial authority. (The cabildo of Concepción ousted a governor of Chile during the seventeenth century.) On this trip to the south Valdivia founded the town of Concepción in March 1550.

There were soon to be more towns. Further expeditions into Araucanian territory brought the founding of La Imperial, Valdivia, and then Villarica. There were also the forts of Arauco, Tucapel, and Purén. By the end of 1553 it appeared as though the Spaniards had established reasonable control over the Araucanian territory.

But a handful of towns and forts were not enough to intimidate the fractious Araucanians. In December 1553 a band of them under the leadership of Lautaro, a youth of about twenty who had been Valdivia's chief groom, destroyed the fort of Tucapel. Valdivia himself marched south with a few dozen of his best troops to deal with the insurgents, but they were all killed by the Araucanians. One could date the commencement of what in Chile is known as the War of Arauco as early as 1536, but it is certain that by the end of 1553 this war was under way. It endured until nearly the end of the nineteenth century and cost tens of thousands of lives on both sides and unmeasured economic losses. Lautaro's uprising was soon generalized and shortly three southern towns, including Concepción, and the three forts were destroyed.

It took until 1557 for Lautaro to be defeated finally. His place was soon taken by Caupolicán, and after his death there would be another Indian leader. Valdivia's place was in turn taken by Villagra, then Hurtado de Mendoza, and so on. The War of Arauco was not always active and hot, but it was always present.

When it flared, towns were destroyed; when it abated, towns were rebuilt and founded. Thus it was that between 1598 and 1612 the seven towns located below the Bío-Bío River—Santa Cruz, Arauco, Angol, La Imperial, Valdivia, Osorno, and Villarica—were destroyed. So costly was the war and so frightening the opponents that the Spaniards resolved to maintain a defensive posture, to fight a holding action, which meant forgoing plans to conquer half of the colony's most fertile land.

After 1612 the War of Arauco was no longer really a war of conquest, but it was nevertheless a war. There continued to be fighting, death, and destruction, and there continued to be a need to hold the frontier through the use of towns and forts. The south of Chile was destined to remain a frontier region until well into the nineteenth century.

The War of Arauco had serious indirect effects on the growth and development of the Chilean nation. Having so awesome an enemy at their southern border forced Chileans into a relatively early although still rudimentary sense of mutual identity, that is, incipient nationhood. Prosecuting the war necessitated social and political stability and demanded at least a basic infrastructure capable of supporting the needs of the frontier towns and garrisons. Finally, the war gave the frontier south its special identity and its willingness and readiness to call out its own troops—its militia—to meet a particular need. Now it was the Araucanians, later it would be Santiago, when the capital blithely thought it could impose its will on the south during the independence period and early nineteenth century.

Not all the natives lived below the Bío-Bío or were Araucanians. Those to the north posed their own problems to the Europeans. It was on the basis of Indian labor in the north and central zones and even in parts of the south that the colony was to be either a success or a failure. Aside from the disinclination of conquerors and later settlers to do tedious manual or other physical labor, there were far too few Europeans or creoles—American-born colonists of European heritage—to supply the quantity of labor necessary to support the colony. Grants of land were made to the conquerors and their troops and to later colonizers, some of which were enormous in size; and grants of Indian labor, the encomienda, were made to provide the labor force. Without Indian labor land or mines were generally useless in early Spanish America.

The encomienda has been one of the most controversial institutions of the colonial period in Spanish-American history. Often it amounted to slavery, always it was a means of exploiting the native population. Though in Chile it was clearly a means of harnessing a vast natural resource of native labor and perhaps making it more productive than it would have been without the encomienda system, it was a means that served principally the *encomendero*, his family, and others like him, rather than the human beings performing the labor. There were indeed exceptions, and at times Indians in encomienda benefited considerably. In 1567, for instance, there were about 150,000 sheep in the vicinity of Santiago, and encomienda Indians owned 50,000 of them. Encomienda Indians in the north and south also owned a variety of livestock.

But ownership of livestock did not lessen the intense physical burden of encomienda labor. The Crown itself feared the total destruction of the native population and took steps to guarantee its preservation and also, therefore, a colonial work force. In 1559 the "measure" of Santillán was decreed in Chile. It was designed to reduce the amount of work required of the encomienda Indian and to protect him from ill treatment, but it was heartily and successfully opposed by the encomenderos. Its need, however, suggests that livestock ownership by Indians in encomienda does not tell the whole story of their general treatment. There were, in fact, other attempts during the colonial period to assuage the plight of the native population, including the abolition of the encomienda system itself; but it was only at the end of the colonial period that the encomienda could be abolished effectively and then because it was no longer as useful and productive a system as earlier.

By the end of the colonial period Chile was governed by an elaborate political system. At the bottom of the vertical structure was the town council, the cabildo. Cabildos, like other governing bodies or officials, could communicate directly with the Crown to redress grievances with higher authorities. During most of the colonial period the provincial governor was called the *corregidor*. At the head of the colonial government stood the governor and captain general. During the seventeenth and eighteenth centuries he was usually known to Chileans as president, indicating his position on the *audiencia*. The audiencia was the supreme court in the colony, but it also possessed certain administrative and consultative duties. The first audiencia was established in 1567 and suppressed only a few years later. It was established permanently in 1609. Toward the end of the colonial period the corregidors were replaced with more powerful and influential intendants. Additionally, during the final phase of the colonial epoch a merchant tribunal, the *consulado,* and a mining tribunal, the *Tribunal de Minería,* were established in Santiago. These were guild-like associations with commanding power and legal jurisdiction over their own members.

Briefly, this was the essential governing structure during much of the colonial period. Distance and the time involved for communication between Crown and colonial governing agency or official, sometimes two or three years, made for a less tightly controlled government than the Crown would have liked. The Crown itself contributed to the diffusion of authority by creating shared and at times conflicting powers and responsibilities in the hope that no colonial agency or official would become powerful enough to threaten royal sovereignty. Generally, efficiency was sacrificed to the goal of loyalty.

2

THE COLONIAL CAPITALIST ECONOMY

Fundamentally, Chile's economy was capitalist during the colonial period. There were clear and significant feudal overtones, such as land usage by small farmers for labor services, but overall the system was one of preindustrial commerical capitalism. Spain itself was centrally capitalist in 1492. The political—though not social—power of the feudal nobility had been broken successfully in Isabel's Castile by the time America was discovered, and it was broken in part by a reliance on an urban counterpoise to the legendary landed aristocracy. Large, dynamic urban centers thrived on commerce, even international commerce, not production to satisfy manorial or village needs. And these urban centers produced a bourgeoisie that was courted by the Catholic kings in their bid to dominate the feudal nobility. In the other major segment of the united monarchy, Ferdinand's Aragon, an urban-based commercial class, a bourgeoisie, had been the ascendant political, social, and economic force for centuries before the colonization of the New World. The Aragonese, in the sense that one may generalize, were traders, while the Castilians, who possessed an ever-growing and powerful commercial class, are more correctly pictured in their pastoral or military pursuits. Remnants of the feudal system existed in Spain in 1492, the most prominent being serfdom, just as feudal modalities would be reproduced over and over again during the colonial and independent histories of the Spanish-American nations. Bearing in mind that economic systems never exist in a pure form, that definitions of them vary and are at best the creation of people's imagination, one may say that Spain was very much an active part of the commercial capitalist world of the late fifteenth century.

Considering that the Catholic kings had taken such pains to

destroy the political power of the territorial nobility, it is not surprising that they would take steps to insure that a feudal nobility
did not become established in the colonies. There was a class
approaching feudal nobility in early Mexico, but this was soon
negated. Nothing approaching a feudal nobility was ever established in Chile. There were about a dozen titles of Castile in Chile
by the end of the colonial period, but these were purchased mostly
by merchants and did not convey political prerogatives.

Chile's economic wealth was in land, commerce, and mining
(though the colony did not possess mines comparable to those in
Peru and Mexico). The gold, silver, and copper mines and the
landed estates, some of which were extremely small even by
modern standards, were dedicated to production for internal and
external markets. Chileans were not producing only to satisfy
estate or local needs, they were producing for a much broader and
promising market; and they were doing so for profit. They may not
have been as profit oriented as modern capitalists, and certainly
some held land essentially for its prestige value rather than for the
amount of profit it could turn, but altogether what we have here is
a system of production and trade.

It was capitalism, but a form that manifested neofeudal overtones. Thus there existed the famous *inquilinos,* small farmers who
received land to use from the estate owner in return for labor
services. There have been examples of *inquilinaje* even in the
twentieth century, although before the end of the nineteenth century there occurred a significant shift to wage payments for labor
services in parts of the country. Recent research has indicated that
some small farmers in Spanish America have been more highly
commercialized and market oriented than the estate owners who
provided their land. It has also been demonstrated that the small
farmers have not always been able to exploit their holdings to the
degree they would like because of the time and energy involved in
fulfilling labor service requirements. This neofeudal remnant of
land usage for labor services has even during the modern period
impeded the full maturing of capitalism in underdeveloped
countries.

The encomienda and the system of large landed estates, called *latifundia,* also conveyed neofeudal overtones. But the encomienda was a grant of Indian labor in the service of production for the world capitalist market. So, too, were latifundia designed for production in the capitalist world. Neither the encomienda nor the latifundia provided the basis of a feudal nobility.

The economic rationale which governed the Spanish colonial system was mercantilism. Although this called for state controls and intervention at all levels of the economy, mercantilism was still centrally capitalism. It was not industrial capitalism of the nineteenth-century variety, though to be successful at mercantilism the mother country would have to manufacture its own goods from colonial raw materials to supply the colonies, nor was it laissez faire capitalism in the Smithian sense, but it was commercialism based on the profit motive and production for distant markets.

However much it was capitalism, mercantilism was still colonialism. Colonies were sought for the benefit of the mother country. The periphery existed for the sake of the metropolis. That the colonies were the personal possession of the Spanish Crown was a technical matter that would have significance at the time of independence: for three centuries they were there to serve Spain. The colonial economic system was headed up by the *Casa de Contratación,* the House of Trade, which supervised all aspects of the colonial economy. What it oversaw was a highly restrictive system designed to insure production of goods in the colonies that would not compete with Spanish production, a plentiful supply of raw materials, a market able to absorb Spanish productivity, and the exclusion of foreigners from the benefits of the colonial system. In fact, the colonies often produced competitive goods and foreigners often benefited by the system either directly through an extensive contraband network or indirectly through Spain itself. Spain lacked the manufacturing base that was mandatory for a mercantilist metropolis, and, after the expulsion of the Jews and final defeat of the Moors (many of whom were bourgeois) in 1492, it also lacked the middle class that might have provided it. Consequently, goods from other European countries were brought into Spain and then transshipped to the colonies. Specie drained out of the mother country, sometimes in voluminous amounts, to pay for the European products. The periphery was certainly serving the metropolis, although the metropolis was not always in Spain.

Spain's inherent limitations as a mercantilist power precluded the possibility of enforcing a thoroughly restrictive economy. Not only was it dependent on the rest of Europe for manufactures, but in times of war Spain had serious trouble supplying the colonies at all. Under these circumstances Spain frequently permitted certain foreign nations to trade directly with the colonies. European goods were usually sent via Spain in the fleet system, the process of sending commercial ships to and from the colonies in regularly scheduled fleets protected by the royal navy. Usually there were two annual fleet sailings, each of which comprised fifty or more ships. One of the fleets sailed for Veracruz and the other for Panama and Cartagena. The merchants would sell their goods at something resembling an annual or semiannual fair and then proceed to Havana for the return trip. The fleet system did, in fact, provide the opportunity for intense supervision and especially the collection of taxes, but it also encouraged trade monopolies and inflated prices. The interminable American coastline, however, the innumerable natural or serviceable ports, and the colonial hunger for cheaper and plentiful European commodities contrived to support a prodigious contraband trade that helped to undermine the economic restrictions of mercantilism and perhaps add enough flexibility to the system for it to endure over the centuries.

Every country has its historical myths. They develop on the basis of partial truths and become ubiquitous in a country's literature—fact and fiction. Sometimes they inspire the populace, sometimes they generate despair. Always they contribute to the national outlook. Chileans have created two fundamental myths about their history. They are (1) that the Chilean economy has been basically feudal, and (2) that the government has been dominated by a powerful landed aristocracy even until very recently. In fact, the Chilean economy has been centrally capitalist, and the government has never been controlled exclusively by a landed aristocracy. To give credence to the newer perspective, several features of the colonial character must be considered.

First is the matter of land division and the territorial aristocracy that developed from it. There were, in fact, many large landed estates in Chile during the colonial period. *Mercedes de tierra,* grants of land, were an obvious and easy way of paying off debts to the conquering soldiers. Some of these grants were truly grand in size. On the basis of these and later grants and purchases a landed aristocracy did come into existence and finally possessed imposing power. There were also *mayorazgos,* entailed estates, that promised continuity of property and, consequently, power.

But it is easy to overemphasize the powers of the owners of entailed estates (also referred to as mayorazgos) and the titled aristocrats. During the seventeenth century 1 mayorazgo was founded and 5 titles of Castile granted. During the final colonial century 16 additional mayorazgos were founded and 7 more titles of Castile granted. Five of the 7 titles of Castile granted during the seventeenth century were purchased by merchants. In a colony in which land was plentiful and cheap a handful of mayorazgos could not control the agricultural or pastoral economy. In fact, there was a continuing process of land division during the colonial period. In the early colonial period, for instance, the region surrounded by the Perquilauquén, Loncomilla, and Maule rivers and the Andes was divided among 5 great estates. These together incorporated hundreds of thousands of acres. But by the end of the eighteenth century there were at least 40 additional landed estates in this same region. Only 13 incorporated more than 4,000 acres, including nonarable land, which was often a high percentage of the total. The remaining estates were smaller, but possessed a larger proportion of arable land. They ranged between 1,600 and 4,000 acres. In estimating social, economic, and political influence these may appear still quite large. But there were also many smaller landed holdings. In 1744 the corregidor of Chillán, in the south, estimated that between the Perquilauquén and Longaví rivers there were 188 farms, of which 36 comprised less than 400 acres. It would be interesting to know just how many small farms existed in the colony. For Chile as a whole there clearly were many farms of less than 1,000 or 1,500 acres, and there were indeed many of less than 200 acres.

In evaluating the influence of the mayorazgos and titled aristocrats, one should bear in mind that neither group acted as a singular force under pressure. Some mayorazgos and titled aristocrats (there were mayorazgos who bore titles also) fought with the patriots during the independence movement, and others were royalists. Nor were their economic interests always harmonious. Regional interests usually superseded what might have developed into a class interest. And this for a very good reason: the needs of southern farmers were often different from those of northern farmers. Crops and market arrangements were not always similar, and the issues of trade or protection and internal improvements struck the individual farmer not by his class orientation but by his personal requirements. Farmers, including the largest and most prestigious, contested farmers in other regions and even within the same region on the basis of their own need to protect products or keep a market open, or to acquire internal improvements. It is not unusual to see a farmer argue during the nineteenth-century transportation revolution against an improvement for another region on the grounds that it might place his locality at a disadvantage. Clearly the legendary landed aristocracy was something less than a cohesive class. The only time the landed rich actually got together along class lines occurred when the institution of mayorazgo was threatened during the early nineteenth century. But even then the issue was highly complex. It is not certain that all the landed rich supported the mayorazgo system, for some surely would have benefited by its destruction. The issue is further complicated during the nineteenth century because mayorazgos theoretically meant more than just rural estates: they signified property, and as such they were also supported by the merchants. Equally as much as the agrarians, merchants were particularly sensitive to the issue of property rights and the personal privilege of passing along an estate to one's heirs.

Even if one were inclined to give the landed interests considerably more credit than is their due for acting as a class or unified group on any issue, there is still the question of placing the Chilean bourgeoisie in the colonial structure. There was not only a dynamic colonial bourgeoisie, it shared power with other elements in the society. And bourgeoisies have had a decided tendency to give their peculiar stamp to the eras in which they lived.

Spain itself displayed a varied society in 1492, and people from all walks of life settled in the colonies during the course of empire. Bourgeois elements found urban centers in which to reside and work. There was trade and mining to occupy them and agriculture, for not a few of the bourgeoisie found their way into the countryside and the agrarian way of life. Since the Spanish bourgeoisie had been fighting for political power for centuries, in some places more successfully than in others, it is not surprising that the colonial bourgeoisie would seek political influence also. And it did so just as effectively as had the Spanish bourgeoisie.

Emphasis on the presence and powers of the landed aristocracy should not distract attention from the impress of the bourgeoisie on Spanish American life during the colonial period or the nineteenth century. The bourgeoisie (the merchants, miners, manufacturers, some bureaucrats and professionals, and even those agrarians who manifested demonstrably bourgeois attitudes and preferences) were functionally dependent on stable governments and the rule of law. They were also dependent on technology and its constant improvement. They lived by profit, sanctified the profit motive, and elevated it to a way of life. The bourgeoisie believed in a society of classes, not estates, but social classes founded on economics. To the bourgeoisie it was imperative that the industrious and talented have access to the whole range of society. It was not a democratic society, but it was patently open by previous feudal standards. It was the bourgeoisie that gave the Western world contractual government; contracts, after all, stood at the very heart of their way of life, Locke's brand of liberalism, and the preference for limited monarchy.

In terms of the entire colonial population the bourgeoisie were few in numbers. Yet they formed the core of the politically active citizenry of the independent Spanish-American nations, including Chile. There are observers who recognize the presence of a large and powerful bourgeoisie in Chile by the end of the colonial period, but they are inclined to believe that society was dominated by a *mixed* bourgeoisie in which the merchants had taken on the central characteristics of the landed aristocracy.[1] There was in fact a mixed bourgeoisie dominant in Chile by 1810, and this is one of the fundamental reasons for Chile's relative stability and progress during the nineteenth century.[2] But it was not a monolithic bourgeoisie. The point is not that the commercial class was absorbed by the landed aristocracy to form a mixed bourgeoisie, but that there existed in Chile by 1810 a bourgeoisie comprised of several key elements in which the commercial class exhibited characteristics that would be more or less identifiable in the tradition of the Western world's bourgeoisies.

Not only was the conquest and colonization of Chile a business venture, but merchants played a significant and visible role from the outset. The first commercial ship arrived from Peru in 1543. Half of its cargo was matériel for Valdivia's troops and half was commercial merchandise. Only three months later a second ship arrived with civilian goods for sale. Trade was conducted among Spaniards and between Spaniards and Indians. The amount of trade being conducted is indicated by a purchase made in Santiago during the early days of the colony for a governor. The governor's majordomo purchased 20,000 pesos worth of a broad category of commodities, including wine, sugar, honey, writing paper, knives, tablecloths, napkins, and wax.

There were notable entrepreneurs among the early settlers. Antonio Núñez de Fonseca arrived in Chile in 1543 or 1544. Before he died he owned the estates called Polpaico, Colina, Lampa, Colmo, and Concón. Using his own ships he conducted trade between Chile and Peru, and he constructed the first ware-

---

[1] The bourgeoisie was *mixed* because of a blending of economic activity and *mixed* because of marriage. Members of the upper bureaucracy and military often married the daughters of leading merchants, miners, and agrarians. This also brought the bourgeoisie into blood relationship with important clergymen.

[2] See especially Alberto Edwards Vives, *La Fronda Aristocrática*, 5th ed. (Santiago, 1959), p. 16.

houses in the port of Valparaíso. He was also involved in ship-building and the fishing industry.

Juan Jufré arrived in Chile with Valdivia and was a distinguished soldier. His military efforts brought him three encomiendas. In 1553 he built a flour mill, and later he added a cloth factory. He was also involved in shipbuilding.

There were many other significant entrepreneurs during the early colonial period. Their ranks were constantly being replenished from within the colony and from abroad. Spaniards and some Portuguese arrived all during the colonial period to conduct their businesses. So too did other Spanish Americans and also some foreigners. Though the Crown tried from time to time to rid the colonies of the foreigners, it was never wholly successful. For instance, there was a brisk direct trade between France and Chile during the early eighteenth century. The French were conducting an illegal trade, but they were there nevertheless. At one point in 1713 there were four French contraband ships anchored at Concepción. Just at the end of the year seven more arrived. French ships traded up and down the Chilean coast, illegally but quite successfully. Small French colonies developed in Concepción, Valparaíso, and Santiago. The French were there to do business, and their skills and determination added markedly to the general growth of the Chilean economy and the bourgeoisie. No matter how the Crown tried to expel foreigners from the colonies, some of the French settlers always managed to stay on; and from their ranks came several of independent Chile's most prominent families.

The ranks of the bourgeoisie were also enlarged by the significant Basque migration to Chile during the eighteenth century. With enviable drive and talent the Basques quickly worked their way up the social, economic, and political ladders. Some entered the colony with little or no capital and amassed impressive fortunes, counted in the hundreds of thousands of pesos. Generally they were involved first in commerce but then also in agriculture. By the end of the colonial period people of Basque origin with names like Amunátegui, Aguirre, Cruchaga, Eyzaguirre, Eguiguren, Echeverría, Larraín, Undurraga, Urrutia, Urmeneta, Urquiza, Vial,

Vicuña, and Zañartu were prominent in Chilean high society. Of the 62 alcaldes in the Santiago cabildo between 1780 and 1811 42 percent were of Basque origin.

One way of determining the presence of a bourgeoisie in colonial Chile is to examine the degree to which merchants achieved political influence. Chile's noted nineteenth-century historian, Diego Barros Arana, while observing that it is not possible to estimate the number of people involved in commerce, does estimate the number of people involved in the *alto comercio,* at the end of the colonial period. By those involved in the alto comercio he means merchants with some capital who legally imported European goods and who supplied the retail merchants. He suggests that there were only about thirty or forty of these and that they resided only in Santiago and Concepción. However, a recent study has concluded that there were more than seventy merchants in the town of Concepción alone, two-thirds of whom might not fit Barros's definition but who had enough capital to import foreign goods, to make profits, to invest and reinvest these profits, and in general to identify with the merchant group. Had there existed a genuine middle class, then some of these merchants might have been members of it; but, given its absence, they were part of the upper class.

It is interesting that many of the leading merchants in the capital of the south of Chile were creoles. Chilean trade was not controlled by *peninsulares,* those born in Spain, as may have been true in some parts of Spanish America. There were indeed prominent and successful peninsular merchants in the colony, most notably perhaps the Basques, but by the end of the colonial period their creole children were often running the businesses.

Some of the southern merchants invested in land, as did their colleagues in the north, especially after 1767 when the Jesuits were expelled and their excellent estates sold at public auction. Of those merchants throughout the colony who did invest in land many continued their central identity as merchants, which is to say that not all merchants who purchased land were absorbed by the attitudes and approaches of the legendary landed aristocracy.

The degree of merchant political influence can be seen in the south. From the early 1780s the town of Concepción was the capital of one of Chile's two intendancies, the other intendancy being the northern one with its capital at Santiago. (Intendants were given local control over justice, general governmental administration, finance, and war.) Once the independence movement commenced, the south became a powerful regional force, at times working harmoniously with Santiago, at times dictating terms, at times standing up to the north militarily. Although there were royal officials who interfered with the political activities of cabildos all throughout the colonies, the town councils still held certain powers which could be employed quite effectively. These might not be powers with generally national significance, but they did directly affect the daily life of local residents.

The town councils have usually been considered the seat of creole political power during the colonial period. It should be noted, however, that many cabildo members were peninsulares. Whether they were European or American the great majority of those in office toward the end of the colonial period continued to live in Spanish America. Although there are no statistical studies, it can safely be assumed that many of these local officials, after dealing with the complicated and ponderous colonial bureaucracy, became fairly effective bureaucrats themselves. In fact, the colonial bureaucracy continued to function after the Chilean independence movement commenced, and it is difficult to find a region, outside a military campaign area, in which the bureaucracy broke down. At times there were spectacular changes of leadership, but the bureaucracy itself continued to function in large measure due to the presence of experienced personnel. One of the reasons for Chile's relatively easy transition from colony to independent nation was the presence of this bureaucracy, key members of which were already quite professional, not only in the sense of being efficient but also in the sense of being full-time public officials, by 1810. Even many of the part-time bureaucrats at the cabildo level had acquired valuable administrative experience that was drawn upon once the independence movement began.

We now have an estimate of the number of merchants in the cabildo of Concepción between 1790 and 1810. This town council was smaller than many in Spanish America. At the end of the colonial period, for instance, it had only about a third as many councilmen, *regidores,* as did the cabildo of Santiago. In this period it usually had four regidores, two alcaldes, a *procurador general,* an *alférez real,* an *alguacil mayor,* an *escribano,* an *alcalde provincial,* and a syndic. The two most powerful figures were the procurador and the alcaldes. The procurador was the town's attorney and was elected annually by the cabildo. He was not legally a voting member of the cabildo and, in fact, was charged with defending the public interest even if it meant arguing against the cabildo. Between 1790 and 1810 65 percent of the procuradores were merchants, that is, people significantly involved in the import-export trade at the wholesale level.

The two alcaldes were the *alcalde de primer voto* and the *alcalde de segundo voto.* The alcaldes were the local justices, with jurisdiction in the first instance in both civil and criminal cases. Even considering how much municipalities differed from each other and from the norms established by the Laws of the Indies, one may label the alcalde de primer voto the most important municipal officer in Concepción, and the alcalde de segundo voto the second most important. Between 1790 and 1810 there were 20 alcaldes de primer voto. Eleven of them were merchants, a total of 55 percent. For the same period there were 21 alcaldes de segundo voto. Seven of them were merchants, a total of 33 percent.

These figures indicate that the Concepción merchants enjoyed impressive political power at the local level. It might be noted that the most important political figure in the south in 1810, Juan Martínez de Rozas, was married to the daughter of José Urrutia y Mendiburu, the south's richest merchant. This marriage made him son-in-law, brother-in-law, and nephew-in-law to probably the leading merchants in the south. For a while after the independence movement started, Rozas controlled the government of Chile.

Not only was there a distinguished merchant class in Chile during the colonial period, there existed also another feature of Western bourgeoisie life—the urban center. Perhaps because Chile has been noted for its agricultural and mining production and its landed aristocracy, the country has appeared to be almost entirely rural. This was not the case even during the colonial period. While recognizing that statistics for the colonial period are far from being as reliable as one would like, Diego Barros Arana has given us some useful ones for the agricultural south. For instance, he estimates that the city of Concepción, the most important political center in the south, had a population of 4,607 people in 1778. In 1790 President Ambrosio Higgins (as he, unlike his son Bernardo O'Higgins, chose to sign his name) estimated that the city had a population of 6,000 prior to an epidemic which took about 1,500 lives. A recent study has shown that the bishopric of Concepción, not including Valdivia, Chiloé, or the Araucanian Indians in the far south (that is, what we might call the south), had a population in 1775 of 77,341. In 1791 it had a population of 103,235. Barros Arana's total for the whole bishopric of Concepción in 1778 is 105,114. Notwithstanding these differences, certain interesting observations may be made. At a time when the bishopric of Concepción is supposed to have had as large a population as 105,114 and the city of Concepción a population of 4,607, that is, following Barros Arana, there were 10 cities in the south with larger populations than the political center. Altogether, the leading 13 urban centers of the south had a population of nearly 68,000 people. That is, more than 50 percent of the southern population lived in urban centers with populations of more than 2,500 people, the figure the 1920 United States Census used as the dividing line between an urban and rural center when it declared the United States more than 50 percent urban. To arrive at the newer estimate of 77,341 we would have to decrease Barros Arana's by about a third. (Barros Arana included some centers that do not figure in the newer estimate, like Valdivia, with a supposed population of 1,879.) If we then took the urban center population of 68,000 and reduced it by a third, the south would still show a decidedly urban population. And this at a time when the city of Santiago had more than 30,000 people.

Surely there are problems here. Probably more people were counted in the cities than in the rural and frontier regions. And in some of the larger urban centers doubtless there were individuals who preferred to count themselves among the city dwellers although they may have spent a good part of the year on their farms. But all in all, it is clear that Chile, and certainly the south, had an advanced urban development at the time of independence. Because towns of 1,000 or 2,000 people or even cities of 5,000 or 6,000 people were often without fine homes or adequate conveniences or health services does not mean that they did not have urban characteristics recognizable in the urban tradition of the Western world. Many of the Chilean towns and cities may have been rural oriented and may have lost much of their populations during the agricultural season, but when we begin to speak of urban centers counting in the thousands, the term "rural" must be used judiciously. Just as large urban centers can manifest rural attitudes, so too can small populations usually referred to as rural manifest emphatically urban attitudes.

The presence of many large urban centers in agricultural and mining Chile suggests that surplus capital produced in the colony ended up in the urban centers. It is popular to maintain that since in capitalism the metropolis supposedly exploits the periphery (even within countries or regions), surplus capital produced in Chile was absorbed by the urban centers before being in turn absorbed by the world metropolises.[3] In fact, the metropolis did not exploit the periphery in Chile so much as this convenient schema would suggest. For one thing, there were scores of urban merchants who bought landed estates. This would be an example of surplus capital flowing back to the countryside. Although there is limited data to guide us here, it would appear that many of the agricultural ventures were drains on the financial productivity of the urban operations.

There is also the matter of the Jesuits. At the time of their expulsion in 1767 the Jesuits were the largest and most successful agrarians in Chile. They owned hundreds of thousands of acres and their haciendas were generally the best run and most produc-

[3] See especially Andre Gunder Frank, *Capitalism and Underdevelopment in Latin America: Historical Studies of Chile and Brazil* (New York, 1969), *passim*.

tive in the colony. Leaving aside the northern mining region of Atacama, since we know very little about the private mining sector during the last century of the colonial period, the Jesuits were the single leading economic power in the private sector. In the whole agricultural sector the Jesuits clearly were the single most potent force. What this means is that to a very significant degree the economic wealth of colonial Chile until 1767 was concentrated in the countryside and not in the metropolis. After 1767 and the sale of the Jesuit estates there was a marked balancing of the colony's wealth between urban and rural regions.

Yet agrarians were still wealthy and after September 1810 would be politically powerful, though not dominant. For instance, it is probable that agrarians not infrequently loaned money to urban dwellers. The case of the wealthy southern landowner, Pasqual Lamilla, is illustrative. He held approximately 62,000 acres of land, and it appears that he made his living essentially from his estates. When he wrote his will in 1805 (he died the following year) he noted that several people owed him money. The merchant Francisco Javier Manzanos, also a leading landowner, owed him 2,000 pesos at the standard rate of 5 percent interest. Alejandro Urrejola, another important merchant-landowner, in association with his son-in-law, the shipowner Manuel de Eguiguren, owed him 3,000 pesos. Juan Felix Manzanos, one of the rare southern lawyers, was another of the important Manzanos family who had to borrow money from Lamilla. Juan Felix had borrowed 500 pesos in silver and had paid back 300 pesos. The magnitude of these loans is indicated by the fact that good rural acreage was selling at considerably less than 1 peso per acre in bulk during the last decades of the colonial period. An individual in the south of Chile with an annual income of between 4,000 and 5,000 pesos was either rich or very close to it. Here we see a landed aristocrat not only financing the economic activities, either directly or indirectly, of two leading merchant-landowners but in a very classic way expropriating their economic surplus. Since both Manzanos and Urrejola and members of their families were active merchants during the late colonial period, one must assume the likelihood that either directly or indirectly their loans allowed them to continue their urban operations as they saw fit. Money was probably flowing from the rural regions to the urban metropolis of Concepción, but it certainly was flowing back to the place of origin with interest.

Not only did colonial Chile have merchants and urbanization, it had a broadly based economy. The commerce mentioned earlier continued throughout the colonial period. By the eighteenth century Chile was conducting a brisk trade with Peru, with Spain, with Buenos Aires, and with the French and other contrabandists. Chile shipped a catalogue of goods—tallow, hides, salted meat, copper, wine, dried fruits, ponchos, and other textiles. Chile also received a wide variety of goods, especially European finished products. The colony was not geographically convenient, but because of its production and needs it was never at any time during the colonial period isolated from the world capitalist market. There were restrictions, but these were largely artificial, created by the mercantilist mother country or local officials. So far from being remote from the world market, Chilean productivity had to withstand the vicissitudes of world competition. As the tempo and horizons of trade increased in the eighteenth century, Chilean producers of ships, rigging, textiles, pottery, metals, and hides often suffered from foreign competition.

Manuel de Salas, the educated and perceptive syndic of the Chilean consulado, once characterized commerce in Chile at the end of the colonial period as "only the art of buying cheap and selling dear." Nothing has done more to perpetuate the myth of a "colonial siesta" than the view of the merchants as being economically passive. This, in turn, has contributed to an underestimation of the numbers and influence of the commercial class in Chile. The Salas description is misleading on at least two counts. First, it disdainfully ignores the dynamism and gratification potentially inherent in every act of buying cheap and selling dear. It haughtily assumes that the act is as simple as the words make it sound, that it is not a complicated and sometimes highly sophisticated endeavor that permits its consummation. And this not merely at the upper levels of merchant society, for one senses that even at the other end of the continuum the less affluent merchants may have had to have been quite diligent and ingenious just to remain in business. And if we were not limiting ourselves to the wholesale and perhaps larger retail operations, we might explore the realities of small shopowning and even peddling.

Salas's comment is misleading also because it incorrectly suggests that the merchants merely sat around waiting for goods and customers. When it came to customers, the merchants may have been in a position to do precisely this; in towns such as Concepción and Valparaíso, which were relatively small among the world's commercial centers, advertisement may not have been demanding. But in importing and exporting the merchants carried on an intense activity. In order to appreciate more accurately the nature of the Chilean bourgeoisie, it is worthwhile to examine some of their economic activities.

One of Chile's most famous merchants during the final phase of the colonial period was the Basque José Urrutia y Mendiburu. He had launched his career in the south of the colony with very limited means, and when he died early in the ninetenth century, he left a fortune of about a half million pesos. At one point he owned (or controlled) three ships carrying wheat from southern Chile to Peru and bringing back sugar and other items. It appears that he purchased his Jesuit estate after making his fortune in commerce, but it is certain that he continued on as a merchant until his death. Another merchant credited him with the development of much of the south's agriculture. Mendiburu's life is not at all the picture of a passive merchant. He was an entrepreneur—wholesaler, shipowner (Chile's largest), and leading agrarian.

Many Chilean merchants had agents in Lima, Buenos Aires, Mendoza, Cádiz, and even London. In 1805 there were about seven Chilean merchants in Spain. But it was not enough for the Chilean merchants to have agents, sometimes brothers or sons, in American and European commercial centers. Early in the nineteenth century there were several attempts to purchase ships for the international trade. This would have given the Chileans far greater control over that trade and a much greater share of the profits. Early in the nineteenth century the brothers Francisco Javier and Ramón Errázuriz, working out of Cádiz, actually had their own ship, the *San Rafael,* but it was captured by the English and seized as war booty. A year later in 1805, the brothers acquired another ship, this one perhaps leased. From Chile the brothers received copper, which they sent to France in 1805 and sold at Bordeaux. Manuel Riesco was another of the Chilean merchants active in the international trade. Though born in Spain, he had settled as a youth in Chile and had earned a fortune. At the end of the colonial period he sent his son Miguel to Buenos Aires and then Cádiz to act as his agent. Not only did Riesco participate in the Chile-Spain trade, sending copper and receiving manufactures, but he dealt with Spanish commercial houses established in London for English goods, especially textiles. In 1805 he instructed his son to lease or purchase a ship for a trip from Spain to Chile. Since his own goods would not fill it, he was instructed to solicit goods from other merchants. To encourage them there would be reductions in freight charges. The ship would sail to Valparaíso, then to Arica, Callao, and Guayaquil, from which point it would begin the return trip. Riesco especially wanted his son to try to have a ship of from 600 to 700 tons constructed. Such a ship built of the best woods with ample storage facilities would cost about 30,000 pesos. To help the financing Miguel would take copper to Santander or Barcelona. Riesco knew of the success the Errázuriz brothers had in selling Chilean copper in France, and he instructed Miguel that if the copper went to Barcelona he should check into prices at Marseilles. All this sounds like active entrepreneurship. The problem was that there was a war going on and Riesco's representatives in Cádiz advised him not to risk such a plan. This was probably good advice; in 1806 the English not only disrupted Spanish trade, they invaded Buenos Aires. But even after the invasion Riesco instructed his son to prepare the lease or purchase of a ship. If the son were successful in this, he would then form a company to carry out trade with Spanish America. It would have a life of at least 10 years and stocks would be valued at 12,000 pesos each. Riesco would take one or two shares for himself and be the Chilean representative; Miguel would be the representative in Lima; and the remaining shares would go to 3 or 4 other merchants. The Napoleonic invasion of the Iberian Peninsula, the elevation of Joseph Bonaparte to the Spanish throne in May 1808, and the subsequent war of reconquest which tore Spain apart obstructed Riesco's plans. But in 1809 he was again determined to continue the project, this time instructing Miguel to look into the possibility of a ship of between 300 and 350 tons in England. The new plan called for Miguel to go to London, where he would purchase textile goods, iron, and tar in addition to the ship. But if it appeared that the entire package could be purchased to better advantage in Sweden, he should travel there to make a deal. If any London merchant wanted to send goods on the ship to Spanish America Miguel should make the arrangements. Once again the unsettled war situation thwarted Riesco's plans, and he had not carried them out by the end of the colonial period. It should be clear, however, that we are speaking of commercial entrepreneurship here and not commercial passivity.

The case of Agustín de Eyzaguirre, one of the leading political figures of the early national period, is also illustrative of this kind of entrepreneurship. Eyzaguirre, a member of one of the colony's most prominent families, started his career as a farmer but turned to commerce, through which he earned a fortune. He had agents in Lima, Mendoza, Buenos Aires, and Cádiz. In 1803 he took advantage of his brother Miguel's study trip to Spain to develop his commercial relations there. At the same time he made contacts through a friend with English merchants. At the end of 1803 he was proposing several alternative commercial plans to Miguel, all of them designed to overcome the grave difficulties caused by international war and official mercantilist policy that presently undermined efforts to send European goods to Chile. The plans could not neutralize these problems, and by 1805 Eyzaguirre also had decided to purchase a ship. But in this desire he was to be just as disappointed as Riesco and for basically the same reason.

There was indeed a powerful bourgeoisie in Chile by the end of the colonial period, and it was not one in which the landed aristocracy predominated and dictated life styles.

There are two features of Chile's colonial capitalist economy that illumine the country's problems as it became independent and threw aside mercantilism. They are the presence of the large neofeudal inquilino class and the immature craft guild development. Both the neofeudal small farmers and the weak and underdeveloped craft guilds were elements that impeded the transition from commercial to industrial capitalism.

Not only were the small farmers who operated on the basis of labor services for land usage prevented from producing as much as capitalism would theoretically suggest, they were long able to remain on the land rather than being forced off it and proletarianized. Had the inquilinos become wage-earning proletarians, they would have been the class to become the core of an industrial proletariat that would have served both as labor force and consumer in the internal market. Even had they remained in the countryside as wage earners and not landholders, the radicalization of the rural regions surely would have taken place long before it did. Small landholders have often been difficult to radicalize, whereas there has generally been less resistance among farm workers.

Strong craft guilds in various European countries contributed to the successful transition from preindustrial to industrial capitalism. Among other things they conferred a high standard of business ethic, and they often were sources of the "original accumulation" that has been requisite for the genesis of industrial capitalism. The Chileans did not have to thwart the powers of craft guilds in the effort to produce cheap, coarse industrial commodities, but neither did they enjoy the benefits of a mature craft guild development.[4]

[4] This is clearly a topic for further study. Our knowledge of craft guilds in colonial Spanish America, specifically, and their relationship to the development first of commercial and then industrial capitalism, generally, is unfortunately limited.

In 1810 Chile had both a colonial and a capitalist economy, but one with striking neofeudal overtones that placed it at a serious disadvantage as it entered the world capitalist market as an independent nation and was forced to compete with the more advanced industrial nations strictly on its own.

3
THE CAUSES OF INDEPENDENCE

The first steps toward independence were taken in Chile as a consequence of Napoleon's seizure of the Spanish throne. Early in May 1808 Napoleon placed his brother Joseph on that throne and thus precipitated a Spanish war of independence. To govern Spain in the absence of the lawful monarch, Ferdinand VII, and to prosecute the war effort, juntas came into existence in various parts of the mother country. Attempting to centralize the war effort the several juntas joined efforts and created a supreme junta in Seville in September. The *suprema* made generally successful attempts to win the support of the colonies. It managed to survive until the French took Seville in 1810 and forced the junta to flee to Cádiz, where it was replaced by a council of regency. The council took control of the Spanish effort and began to rule in the name of Ferdinand. One of its most significant early acts was to call for the convening of a parliament, a *cortes,* to which the colonies were invited to send delegates.

Legally the colonies belonged not to Spain but to the Crown of Castile, which meant that in the absence of the lawful monarch the colonies technically had the right to establish their own juntas to govern in the name of Ferdinand. Between 1810 and 1814, when Ferdinand regained the Spanish throne and proclaimed the reestablishment of royal absolutism, several of the colonies established governing juntas and grew dangerously accustomed to the privilege of what amounted to self-government. With the restoration of Ferdinand they chose formal independence rather than submit to Spanish rule. Chile was one of them.

Chile's first national junta was established by a cabildo abierto in Santiago on September 18, 1810. The junta was something less than the radical governing body later patriots gave it credit for being. The cabildo abierto, comprising several hundred people, elected Mateo de Toro Zambrano president of the junta. Toro Zambrano was the recently appointed captain general of the colony. Born in Santiago some eighty years earlier, he had been a successful merchant and was presently one of Chile's most important landowners. He bore the title Conde de la Conquista. For vice president the cabildo abierto chose José Antonio Martínez, the bishop-elect of Santiago. Originally the body of the junta was supposed to comprise three *vocales*. Fernando Márquez de la Plata, a peninsular from a prominent Spanish family and himself an important government official, was chosen first vocal. Juan Martínez de Rozas from Concepción was elected second vocal. A leading landowner, Ignacio de la Carrera, was chosen third vocal. The people attending the cabildo abierto wanted to elect two additional vocales; consequently, on a second vote Francisco Javier Reina, a soldier and loyal supporter of the Crown, and Juan Enrique Rosales, related to the powerful Larraín family, were chosen.

It was really a rather respectable body chosen that day to govern the colony in the name of the deposed king. Self-government proved addictive, however, and for the privilege the colony fought a war with the viceroyalty of Peru in 1813. The Peruvians invaded Chile in that year and defeated the Chileans in 1814. The viceroy of Peru controlled the colony until 1817, when it was liberated by José de San Martín.

There were many characteristics of the Spanish colonial system that might have induced an independence movement in Chile, but none of them actually did until the Napoleonic invasion of Spain gave the Chileans the opportunity of governing themselves. Nevertheless, these characteristics impelled many Chileans toward independence after the establishment of the national junta. In a sense, then, they prepared the way for Chilean independence.

The most meaningful context in which to view the characteristics of the colonial system that prepared the way for an acceptance of independence after 1810 and even led some Chileans, like Bernardo O'Higgins and Juan Martínez de Rozas, to favor independence long before the establishment of the first national junta, is the European Enlightenment. The Enlightenment was too much a part of the Western way of life during the last decades of the eighteenth century for it to be kept out of the colonies. The Crown and church prohibited the importation of the more radical tracts into the colonies, but the Enlightenment was a way of thinking, a way of looking at things, and as such it transcended artificial barriers. It was Cartesian rationalism, a belief in progress and the perfectability of humanity, it was the modern scientific approach to problems. When the Crown encouraged scientific improvements and education, as it did vigorously during the late eighteenth century, it encouraged Enlightenment thinking.

In political theory the Enlightenment meant different things to different people. To some it meant limited monarchy, to others, enlightened despotism. To some it meant, perhaps, Locke's property oriented, individualistic liberalism, to others, Rousseau's liberalism of the people—his democracy. While the overwhelming majority of the Chileans who were to become the active citizenry of the new nation were Lockean liberals, there were a few Rousseauian democrats around. Thus, there occurred the conspiracy of the *Tres Antonios* in 1780. Though it finally failed, this conspiracy was a serious attempt to overthrow the colonial government and actually revolutionize society. The three Antonios, Antonio Gramusset and Antonio Berney, both French, and José Antonio de Rojas, the prominent Chilean they had enlisted in their ranks, proposed the establishment of a republican government founded on the most progressive electoral process. Not only would slavery have been abolished, but social classes would have been eliminated. Their plans called for an advanced program of agricultural reform as well as a broad policy of free trade with markets outside the empire.

Apart from science the area in which the Enlightenment most closely approached liberalism was economics. Although the ultimate goal of the Spanish reformers was to strengthen the empire and revitalize the mercantile system, they did, in fact, liberalize aspects of the trading system by lessening many restrictions. By 1810 a local variety of Smithian economics (incorporating protectionism) and Lockean politics had fused into an appealing combination that informed the liberalism of the active citizenry in Chile and the other newly independent Spanish American nations. The Enlightenment did not directly cause the Chilean independence movement. Yet, it started people thinking and it gave them ideas. This proved detrimental to the concept of empire.

The Enlightenment led to the so-called Bourbon reforms, established by the Crown to strengthen its authority, to increase its revenues, to protect the empire from foreign intrusion, and to assuage some of the complaints raised by colonists that might cause rebellion. Though the reforms did not of themselves cause the independence movement, they did cause self-government to be highly attractive to many colonists after the Napoleonic invasion of Spain.

The two most famous of the Bourbon reforms were the expulsion of the Jesuits and the establishment of free trade. The Jesuits were expelled from the colonies in 1767 as part of the Crown's attempt to enhance its own prerogatives and reinforce royal absolutism. The Jesuits had become something of a state within a state and were a distinct challenge to the concept of enlightened despotism. There were other prominent orders in Chile: the Dominicans, Franciscans, and Augustinians, but the Jesuits were the richest and most powerful. Not only did they possess immense agricultural and pastoral holdings, they were involved in a wide variety of related manufacturing ventures. When they were expelled, their estates and businesses were sold at public auction. Consequently, quite a few Chileans now had the opportunity of acquiring estates that were among the best-managed and most productive in the colony. It was precisely at this time that many of the famous landowning merchants of the late colonial period purchased their estates. Clearly not all Chileans were sorry to see the Jesuits go. Members of the other orders, who had become over the centuries natural competitors of the Jesuits, were not particularly sorry. Nor was the secular hierarchy, since the Jesuits competed with it for power and prestige.

But the expulsion of the Jesuits was indeed a vigorous attack on the church and doubtless induced some clergymen to consider the benefits of independence. There were, in fact, some notable clerics throughout the colonies who favored independence prior to the Napoleonic invasion. There was, naturally, Hidalgo of Mexico. Bernardo O'Higgins, as a young student and already a dedicated separatist, met two Spanish-American clerics in Spain who favored independence years before the elevation of Joseph Bonaparte to the Spanish throne. One was the Argentine Juan Pablo Fretes, who later became canon of the cathedral of Santiago and a president of Chile's first national congress. There is no telling just how much the Crown's attack on the church influenced the radicalization of these clerics. There were also Jesuits in exile, like Juan Pablo Viscardo, who propagandized boldly and eloquently for Spanish-American independence.

Ultimately the expulsion of the Jesuits had far deeper meaning in Chile than merely encouraging a few colonists along the road to independence. The expulsion turned over a veritable economic empire to Chilean commercial and agrarian interests. Not only were the economic resources of the Chilean social groups that were soon to lead the colony into nationhood now visibly and impressively enhanced, there also occurred a meaningful change in the nature of those social groups. Leading commercial interests now had a new and excellent opportunity of becoming agrarian interests also. The endeavors and horizons of the Chilean commercial class were infinitely expanded.

The Crown's interference with the colonial economy—its liberalization of many mercantile restrictions—during the final century of empire was potent medicine in rendering independence more palatable than it might have been otherwise to many Chileans once the national junta was established in 1810. The most spectacular royal economic reform of the late colonial period was the famous freedom of trade decree of 1778. The decree officially opened many ports in Spain and America to trade within the Spain-American axis. Valparaíso and Concepción were among them. From this date these two Chilean ports were permitted officially to trade directly with thirteen Spanish ports and many other Spanish-American ports. Some tariffs were reduced and in general emphasis was placed on facilitating commerce within the empire. The colonial trade monopoly that favored the Seville-Cádiz merchants was consequently ended.

The Crown's ultimate goal was not merely to liberalize the imperial trading system, but to strengthen it. Thus, at the same moment it could reduce certain restrictions, the Crown could institute a powerful monopoly on tobacco, the *estanco*. The Crown wanted increased revenue from trade, and this it got from the liberal trade reforms. Increased revenue resulted not so much from expanding the total amount of trade, however, as from expanding legal trade. The new reforms left the extensive and rewarding contraband trade less attractive than previously.

Actually, the 1778 decree was not as eventful in Chile as elsewhere. In reality the decree merely legalized an already existing situation. In 1720 the crown permitted the use of *navíos de registro,* ships that traveled independently of the fleet system to specified ports under special license. The purpose of the new system was to take care of the needs of ports that could not be satisfied by the traditional commercial system. Rather than preserving the viability of the old fleet system, the registered ships were so successful in supplying Spanish-American markets that they made the fleets obsolete. The war between England and Spain that started in 1739 and endured about a decade gave further priority to the registered ships. The fleet system received additional setbacks by the war in general and the destruction of the port of Portobelo by Admiral Vernon in particular. In 1740 the navíos de registro were permitted to travel directly between Spain and Chile around Cape Horn. The first ships making the trip around the Cape had great successes.

Not only was the Chilean market supplied, however, once the registered ships began arriving, it became oversupplied. Letters written from Chile to Spain in 1761 make it quite evident that the local market was flooded: some goods could not be sold and others could be sold only at cost. In 1769 a merchant wrote from Santiago of the hapless state of commerce due to the abundance of clothing goods and the scarcity of silver. Yet many merchants traded a broad range of goods and were thus generally able to make some sort of profit and keep their operations going. The situation continued on into the 1780s. In 1786 a ship arrived in Valparaíso from Cádiz and to sell its cargo had to offer credit of a year and a half on prices that were so low as to eliminate competition. The result was that prices on these goods were as low as in Cádiz itself. That same year a merchant arrived with goods from Buenos Aires but so flooded was the Chilean market that he had trouble selling them. He had to return some goods to Argentina.

In 1787 the crown ordered the president of Chile to investigate the state of the colony's commerce. Higgins made his report in 1789. It is a well-known and often quoted statement, one that recounted the sorry state of Chilean commerce. Higgins had asked several merchants to make their own observations on the state of Chile's commerce. Domingo Díaz de Salcedo y Muñoz noted that the Chilean market was so supplied with European goods, "that for not being able to digest its excessive intake the body politic is considered mortally sick and in extreme need of a long convalescent diet." Francisco Javier Errázuriz considered the central problem with Chilean commerce to be an excessive amount of free trade. The whole commercial community, he observed, clamors against the new system of free trade. Errázuriz did not want to see an end to the system, rather, he wanted it regulated. Instead of permitting ships to arrive in Chile as often and whenever they wished, they should be allowed in only according to a plan that would enable the local merchants to regulate their operations.

Another merchant, José Urrutia y Mendiburu, noted the great excess of European goods. The Concepción market was so satiated that of a cargo worth 100,000 pesos or more only 40,000 or 50,000 pesos worth could be sold in a period of 3 to 4 years and with a profit of only 12 or 14 percent over the cost in Spain.

These reports and letters make it patently clear that what the Chileans required was not more free trade but the privilege of directing their own economic affairs. This impression is conveyed further in a request made by Mendiburu in 1800. This rich and powerful southern merchant, shipowner, and landowner requested permission to send ships laden with Chilean goods from Talcahuano to the Philippines. The south of Chile was fertile, he observed, but poor because it lacked facilities to export its abundant produce. He believed that the Philippines needed what Chile could supply. Mendiburu took pains to show that everyone concerned, even the Crown, would benefit directly from the privilege. The intendant of Concepción, Luis de Alava, supported the request, observing that the plan was of supreme utility for stimulating the agriculture of the colony, which "abounds with produce and only lacks places to supply with its abundance."

There were several interesting official opinions presented in reference to the Mendiburu solicitation. The merchant association—the consulado—requested the opinion of a merchant who, while not opposed to the idea of such trade in principle, argued that it should be carried out from the port of Valparaíso and should not be the monopoly of one person. In this we see that Chilean federalism had strong and distinct economic roots dating back to the colonial period. The syndic of the consulado asked the administrator of the aduana to report on how such trade would affect revenue. He vigorously supported Mendiburu's plan on the grounds that the proposed trade would be very beneficial to the royal treasury. He repeated what by 1800 had become a familiar argument: that Chile really only needed to increase the export of its "abundant and rich produce" in order "to move rapidly toward opulence." And this *"grandeza* would not be stretched out on weak and false foundations, but on the most solid and permanent, which is agriculture." The problem in Chile, he noted, was the lack of commerce.

One point raised by the administrator is of special interest. He observed that during the present four years of war with England, Chile had fallen into a "state of astonishing scarcity of all European goods and effects." Merchants had even been forced to take merchandise from their own shelves to clothe themselves and their families. This is quite a reversal of the situation that had existed a decade earlier. The solution now was not less freedom of trade but more of it.

Though it is not known whether Mendiburu received his privilege, it is certain that the matter of free trade, that is, whether to have more or less of it at any given moment, was a fundamental problem of the late colonial period.

Another example of the free trade controversy is the Peruvian shipping monopoly of the eighteenth century. The shipping monopoly was created and sustained artificially. It existed because the viceroy of Peru would allow few non-Peruvian ships to bring Chilean exports into Peru and because the Crown would not permit the Chileans to trade in the world capitalist market as freely as many articulate Chileans desired, especially during the final decades of the colonial era.

The trade monopoly was based on Peruvian need of Chilean wheat. A devastating earthquake in 1687 played havoc with Lima's wheat fields and forced an immediate Peruvian dependency on Chilean agriculture. From the end of the seventeenth century Chilean wheat displaced its Peruvian competitor because it was cheaper to produce. Chilean wheat producers were clearly exploited by the Peruvian shippers, who maintained both an informal and formal trade monopoly over Chilean wheat.

The formal monopoly was founded on both royal and viceregal legislation. The viceroy of Peru ruled that Chilean wheat could be brought to Callao only in Peruvian ships. Thus by fiat the basis of the trade monopoly was created. But the viceregal decree was not aimed at Chilean shippers, who were exceedingly few, so much as Guatemalan and other shippers of Chilean wheat. At one point during the last decade of the eighteenth century twenty-six ships worked the Peru-Chile trade, of which only three were owned by Chileans. In the middle of the eighteenth century royal legislation that had restricted Chilean shippers from trading all the way up the Pacific coast to Panama was removed. Theoretically, the Chilean merchants no longer were subject to the monopoly of the Peruvian merchants. But by the middle of the eighteenth century Peru was the natural market for Chilean products, and the Chileans did not possess enough ships to take worthwhile advantage of the more liberal trade policy.

The informal monopoly worked this way. The owners of the warehouses, the *bodegas,* in Valparaíso were theoretically the agents of the producers, but in reality they stored the wheat and sold it to their own advantage. That is, they could drive the price either up or down. Hence, they were exploiters. Then they in turn had to sell the wheat to the Peruvian shipowners, who, banded together, were in a position to establish an artificial ceiling on the price they paid the bodegueros. The final factor is that Chile was not only the natural producer of Peru's wheat, but, so long as Peruvians largely controlled Chile's export capability, the wheat would go to Peru. And there the sale of the wheat generally was in Peruvian hands.

The trade monopoly was opposed not only by many Chileans, including producers of wheat, government officials, and the Santiago cabildo, all of whom attempted to undermine the practices of the Valparaíso bodegueros and their deals with the Peruvian shipowners, but also by many Peruvians. Lima breadmakers were appalled by the trade monopoly, which artificially inflated the price of wheat and bread. They even planned to import Chilean wheat themselves, but at this they eventually failed. They made efforts to encourage local farmers to produce more and cheaper wheat.

Even the viceroy himself saw grave dangers in the trade monopoly. To insure a supply of wheat for Peru and lessen its dependency on Chile he instituted a policy called *preferentismo,* a preferential policy which called for the purchase of Peruvian-produced wheat before imported wheat, and the establishment of price ceilings on Chilean wheat. Thus a drop in the price of Chilean wheat during the 1750s has appeared to have been the result of a superabundance of Chilean wheat and a lessened Peruvian demand. This would suggest a classical example of the inequitable workings of the world capitalist market. The periphery, Chile, had grown accustomed to producing for the metropolis, Lima, and now suffered the consequences of the vagaries of the world capitalist market. Actually the problem for Chilean producers of wheat was not caused by the free functioning of the market system, but by internal Peruvian factors, that is, the strenuous efforts of the viceroy to lessen Peruvian dependency on Chilean wheat and to lower local prices.

This impediment thrown in the way of the open market system by the viceroy led to an interesting result. High government officials in Chile and the Peruvian shipowners both began to argue for free trade. President Amat of Chile and the Peruvian shipowners both presented cases to the viceroy arguing that his policy of *preferentismo* would ruin the merchant marine of the west coast of southern South America. It is ironic that the Peruvian shipowners, who thrived on a virtual monopoly of shipping Chilean wheat, should now become free traders.

Yet while some Chileans must have thought prior to September 1810 that they should be creating and administering their own economy, one that would be more attentive to the colony's needs, it appears that most did not come to this conclusion until after the independence movement had gotten under way, that is, until after Chileans were running their own economy anyway.

Free trade did not cause independence, though it certainly converted many Chileans to the idea of self-government between 1810 and 1813. The Chileans promulgated a free trade decree of their own in February 1811 which amply demonstrates that the issue was not freedom of trade but the need of a local economy to be governed locally. The free trade decree of February 1811 not only liberalized Chilean trade, it incorporated a considerable amount of protectionism, and it raised tariffs overall approximately two-thirds. Certain articles could not be imported at all, and others might be excluded in the future to promote the country's industry.

In February 1811 the Chileans manifestly took on the task of administering their own economy. They desired to trade with whomever they chose and at the same time to promote their own manufacturing and agricultural base. They had been limited in both areas by Spanish policy and clearly could not strike a promising balance between trade and protection. Now they were not as successful as they might have desired, but this is another story. The point here is that between 1810 and 1813 quite a few Chileans shifted toward independence in part owing to the benefits of a locally administered economy.

Two other Bourbon reforms influenced the disruption of the Spanish empire in America. One was the intendancy system, established first in Cuba in the 1760s and then transferred to the rest of the colonies. Chile was divided into two intendancies in 1786. The Chilean intendants were all peninsulares (European-born Spaniards), who replaced previous provincial governors (often creoles) while enjoying much greater power than their predecessors. Sometimes these Spaniards stimulated local economies and, as in the case of Mendiburu and Luis de Alava, supported the needs of leading residents. But at other times they interfered in local affairs, attacked traditional privileges, and alienated prominent families. Thus between 1789 and 1796 the intendant of Concepción fought an intense legal battle to remove members of two leading families from the town council. The intendant felt that the families had too much representation in the council. He was not quite successful and managed to antagonize a good many people. At times intendants won friends, as in the case of the Mendiburu petition, but at other times they antagonized important creole families. Though intendants must be credited with having done some good for the colonial system, they probably also encouraged not a few powerful colonists to contemplate the benefits of independence.

The second of the remaining consequential Bourbon reforms was the creation of creole regular army units and the expansion of the creole militia, both with creole officers. One of the fundamental goals of the Bourbon reforms was to defend the colonies against foreign incursion. To do this effectively with peninsular troops, as the Crown probably would have liked since the armies then would have been reliable in the event of colonial rebellion, would have entailed a prodigious financial outlay just when the Crown was attempting to increase its revenues. The Chilean militia with its creole officers numbered in the tens of thousands. It was a reform that delighted the creoles, especially the officers. They not only got their uniforms, they were entitled to the *fuero*, the privilege of special military jurisdiction for themselves and their families, enjoyed by the regular army. The reform was altogether a form of recognition for the creole population. And while it may have endeared many to the colonial system, we are left with the immutable fact that the Crown had thus created the future patriot armies.

There is one final aspect of late colonial life that is generally considered a cause of independence. That is the competition between creoles and peninsulares for public office. The importance of this competition which did, in fact, exist was blown out of proportion during the independence movement itself and during the early national period. Though there was no legal distinction between creoles and peninsulares for public office, peninsulares clearly enjoyed preferential treatment when it came to the highest posts. Socially, peninsulares in Chile enjoyed no particular advantage over creoles, they managed to get into whatever social grouping their position or talents entitled them to. In some areas there indeed was a heated creole-peninsular competition, the most notable being within the religious orders. Though some Chileans complained about the prevalence of peninsulares in public office, most do not seem to have been very concerned about the matter. In fact, in 1810 the upper Chilean bureaucracy was very much a creole affair. At the time the national junta was created the interim governor and president was a creole, as were the bishop-elect of Santiago, two judges of the royal audiencia, the superintendent of the royal mint, the administrator of the aduana, and the *asesor,* the chief counsel in the colony. However, there is no doubt that the peninsular intendants alienated some creoles from the colonial system strictly on the basis of their having been peninsulares.

There was a creole-peninsular competition in late colonial Chile, but it was a competition that grew in dimension and meaning after the establishment of the national junta, that is, after

Chileans were appointing or electing whomever they chose to public office.

The Chilean society that was to see its imperial structure seriously subverted in 1808 and create its own alternative governing mechanism in 1810 was not entirely static. It was a bourgeois society that had to remain relatively open to avoid stagnation. Merely the influx of the industrious and successful Basques and French during the eighteenth century would have frustrated a static and closed society. This is not to suggest that members of the upper classes were not jealous and protective of their position or that those of the lower were not unaware of the fact that they were clearly not in the upper reaches of society and that the gulf which separated them, which isolated them from obvious special privileges, was terribly difficult to overcome.

Not only was society less than static, in some places it was in a state of flux. During the latter part of the eighteenth century one of the Bourbon reforms contributed to further urbanization in Chile. In an effort to hold frontier regions against foreigners and Indians, urban centers were artificially established. Among those towns founded by fiat in the south of the colony during the eighteenth century were Quirihue, Colemu, Los Angeles, Florida, and Cauquenes. There were many smaller ones, but these 5, according to the official estimate of 1778, contained a population of 30,993, that is, more than a quarter of the southern population. Some of these new urban centers supported populations two or three times as large as Concepción's, according to the 1778 estimate. These new towns, as well as the older ones, contributed to social mobility in the south of Chile. The creation of municipalities in Chile as a whole led to a depopulation of the agricultural regions and a consequent shortage of agrarian workers, much to the chagrin of the hacendados. And since not all the new urban dwellers could be absorbed into the local economies, bands of vagabonds and thieves began to appear, some of them doing extensive damage. Feeding this general trend was a rapidly growing population. The annual rate of population growth in the bishopric of Concepción (excluding Valdivia, Chiloé, and the lands controlled by the Araucanians) between 1755 and 1812 was 3 percent. This was very high. For the same period the bishopric of Santiago shows a rate of population growth of between 1 and 2 percent annually. Between 1700 and 1834 the bishopric of Santiago had an average annual population growth of 1.7 percent, while for the same period that of Concepción shows an average of 3 percent. To put it another way, between 1719 and 1812 the population of the bishopric of Concepción doubled every 25 years.

The new urbanization, the rapidly growing population, the openness of society at the top, and the limited opportunity facing the overwhelming majority of the population at the bottom together might properly have placed Chile in a clear pre-revolutionary mold by 1810. What it got, however, was not a revolution but a change in government.

PART II
THE NINETEENTH CENTURY

4

THE ESTABLISHMENT OF THE
LIBERAL NATION

Chile's early national history may conveniently be divided into four distinct chronological periods. The first commences with the establishment of the national junta in September 1810 and terminates with the defeat by the viceregal forces in 1814. This period in Chilean history is known as the *patria vieja*. The second period is that of reestablished royal authority in 1814 until the patriot invasion in 1817. The third period begins with the spectacular entrance of San Martín's Army of the Andes into Chile and the subsequent election of Bernardo O'Higgins to the supreme directorship in 1817 and ends with the supreme director's resignation in early 1823. The final period begins with the fall of O'Higgins and runs to the victory of the so-called *pelucón* coalition in 1829. It is sometimes referred to as the period of anarchy or chaos in Chilean history.

The period of the patria vieja is one of the most interesting and episodic in Chilean history. Clearly it started out for most as a patriotic venture in the name of the deposed king, Ferdinand VII, but for many it ended as a patriotic venture in the name of Chile. So many significant events took place in just a few years that life must have been very exhilarating to the active citizenry. In 1811 the free trade policy was established and a national congress convened. Though the Chileans were entirely competent to administer governments, counting among their number several highly experienced and qualified bureaucrats, they were not at all sure how to go about running a congress. But after some initial difficulties, they got the congress going. In September 1811, however, José Miguel Carrera forcefully took control of the congress. Before he was twenty-six Carrera dominated the government of Chile. He was one of the more progressive of the early national leaders and under his tutelage the congress became a source of advanced legislation. Regional interests felt threatened by his activities in Santiago, however, and consequently provincial juntas came into existence. The most important was the junta of Concepción. The south, in fact, prepared to go to war with Santiago, but it was at this juncture that an invasion force sent by the viceroy of Peru landed in the south. Although many Chileans fought with the royalists, the governments and armies of the provinces of Concepción and Santiago joined in the effort to preserve what was rapidly becoming the independent nation of Chile.

It took the Peruvians only between March 1813 and October 1814, at the Battle of Rancagua, to defeat the Chileans. The period of self-government was ended and the idea of a Chilean nation dealt a mournful blow. For three years while the independence movement was in a state of limbo Chilean refugees in Argentina planned their triumphant return. Some arrived back home as part of San Martín's combined Army of the Andes in February 1817, which quickly and easily defeated the royalist defenders at Chacabuco, to the northeast of Santiago, and then entered the capital.

From early 1817 until early 1823 Bernardo O'Higgins was the supreme director of Chile. Independence was declared and a provisional constitution promulgated. O'Higgins, the illegitimate son of an Irish president of Chile and viceroy of Peru, was one of colonial Chile's first and most dedicated separatists and the ranking Chilean in the Army of the Andes. His arrival augured the establishment of a firm and stable government that would promise continuity, but Chilean politics required a more sensitive guiding hand. In Catholic Chile he attacked the church, imprisoning friars and even exiling the bishop of Santiago. He attacked the privileges of the landed rich at a time when their adhesion to the early national regime might have been more in the interests of the country. His short-lived constitution of 1822 challenged the powers of the provinces in a country in which the northern and southern provinces were intensely jealous of their prerogatives.

Whether or not he had alienated the provinces O'Higgins might have had a difficult time maintaining power. Though a great

Chilean patriot he represented the Argentine grand scheme of liberation of the continent. The liberation of Chile had been only a necessary stepping stone on the way to Peru. Not only did the Chileans owe an overwhelming debt to the Argentines for their independence, but between 1817 and 1820 (when San Martín departed for Peru), the government of Chile was in a very real sense managed by Argentine interests. The controlling power in the early O'Higgins administration was the secret *Logia lautarina*. This was the Chilean branch of the secret lodges dedicated to the liberation of Spanish America founded in London by Francisco Miranda and in Buenos Aires by José de San Martín. Since the Chilean lodge was secret also, we cannot properly judge its accomplishments or even know who belonged to it. It is clear, however, that San Martín, O'Higgins, other leading militarists, and important government officials belonged. No act of government, no appointment of important or even moderately important civil, religious, or military officials could be made without lodge approval. The *Logia lautarina* was indeed a powerful supragovernmental agency. It contributed mightily to the presence of a decidedly Argentine air in the upper reaches of Chilean government and as such served to remind knowledgeable Chileans of their debt to the Argentines and the influence of foreigners in their government. Once San Martín took his *Expedición Libertadora* to Peru in August 1820 the lodge ceased to possess significant power, but by then the damage already had been done to O'Higgins's image. By 1820 in the face of growing Chilean nationalism O'Higgins had begun to appear to many Chileans as less the great Chilean patriot and more the representative of the Argentine independence movement. The foreign influence in the O'Higgins government alone might have proved troublesome eventually, but coupled with the supreme director's attack on the church, the landed aristocracy, and then the provinces, it could do little less than cause his failure.

A provincial rebellion that started in the south impelled O'Higgins to resign in January 1823. O'Higgins was replaced by Ramón Freire, who led the southern rebellion. During the next seven years Chile had many governments and presidents. In one two-year period alone the presidency was occupied by Francisco Antonio Pinto, Francisco Ramón Vicuña, Francisco Antonio Pinto, Vicuña again, Ramón Freire, Francisco Ruiz Tagle, José Tomás Ovalle, and Fernando Errázuriz. There was a constitution in 1823 that attempted to regulate public and private opinion and one in 1828 that had democratic overtones. There was a federalist movement which culminated in 1826 in the establishment of a short-lived federalist republic. It seemed as if there was a bit of just about everything during these seven turbulent years.

There was turbulence and at times the impression of chaos, but there was no anarchy. The changes in organic codes, the frequent changes in administrations certainly were confusing and at times disruptive to the ordinary and efficacious functioning of government, but overall the lives and economic activities of few people were affected. Nevertheless, there was an instability that did not harmonize with the fundamental interests of the Chilean bourgeoisie. In 1829 the pelucón coalition seized control of the government and provided the stability that would distinguish Chile among the Spanish-American countries during the nineteenth century.

The term "oligarchy" should be used with great care when dealing with Chile's early national history. There was indeed an inordinately powerful and prestigious group of families, perhaps 100 or so, at the time of independence that resembled an oligarchy. However, this group of families formed part of an active citizenry that was noticeably larger and more open than an oligarchy. At the time of independence there were somewhere between 500,000 and 800,000 people living in non-Araucanian Chile. The majority of Chileans, hundreds of thousands, were part of the inert masses who did not enjoy the franchise. But at the other end of the continuum stood the active citizenry, whose numbers it is impossible to estimate accurately but who surely could be counted in the thousands, who were able to vote and hold office. For the Chilean active citizenry society was quite open and dynamic, and anyone just reaching its lower ranges could hope through hard work, talent, and luck to reach the top.

The active citizenry was a mixed merchant-mining-agrarian bourgeoisie, elements of which were more or less bourgeois than others. Though there were a few democrats in the active citizenry, most were classical liberals of the Lockean and Burkean schools. Far from being democrats, they were fearful of democracy and dismayed by the excesses of the French Revolution. Theirs was a society of individuals banded together to protect property rights. For society as a whole the will of the majority was threatening and they designed organic codes to prevent the majority from gaining power. Yet the active citizenry itself was strikingly pluralistic and its government highly representative of the enfranchised population. Later on in the nineteenth century when voting qualifications were lowered, governments for many decades were less representative of the enfranchised population. Many thousands of people were then given the franchise, but their votes were largely controlled and the effect of enfranchisement rendered meaningless.

In modern terms the active citizenry was exceedingly conservative. Yet the active citizenry was not all of one voice on critical issues. Some were free traders, others, protectionists. Bernardo O'Higgins attacked the church, Diego Portales supported the church and used it pragmatically as a bulwark of political stability. O'Higgins governed with the military at his side, Portales weakened the powers of the military and created a civic militia as a realistic counterweight to its powers. At the founding of the nation the issue of monarchy was not very serious. As classical liberals the active citizenry for the most part would have been just as comfortable under a limited constitutional monarchy as under a constitutional republic. Altogether the issue of monarchy was more interesting to Chileans for its value as a diplomatic tool, a bargaining agent, than as an ideological debate.

Much can be learned about Chile's active citizenry from its constitutions. The country's first constitution, a provisional code, was issued in 1812. Executive authority was established in a three-member junta and pointedly limited by a seven-member senate. As early as 1812 we see the beginnings of a notable and yet often unnoticed trend in Chilean constitutional history: executive power was balanced by strong congresses. By 1812 Chile was divided into three provinces—Concepción, Santiago, and Coquimbo. Santiago was permitted three senators and the other two provinces, two each. The northern and southern provinces, Coquimbo and Concepción, had effectively insured that the central province, Santiago, would not—as it desired—dominate the new government. The junta required senatorial approval on all important matters, such as declaring war, effecting a peace, coining money, establishing alliances and treaties of commerce, naming envoys, moving troops, and altering the constitution. All faculties not expressly declared in the document were reserved to the sovereign public. There would be freedom of press, but so that this freedom would not degenerate into license, the junta and senate would prescribe rules of conduct.

Typical of the early Chilean classically liberal approach was the article which stated that all free Chileans were equal before the law, with only merit and virtue causing one individual to be more suitable for public office than another. This was a sincere expression of the active citizenry's conception of society. Individual members of that citizenry doubtless considered merit and virtue not at all restrictive to their group as a whole. At this date in Chilean history it was not yet a question of whether a domestic servant possessed the characteristics requisite for office-holding. Because of the war against the viceroy's forces, which commenced the following year, the constitution was unexpectedly short-lived.

Chile's next constitution, also a provisional document, was promulgated in 1818 after independence was declared. Chileans were very much aware of the United States constitution: a United States consul, Joel Roberts Poinsett, had even presented Carrera his personal draft of one for Chile, one that would have made it impossible at that time for the man who controlled the government of Chile, Carrera, to become president because of his youth. It was rejected. For their constitutionalism Chileans turned to the liberal Spanish Cádiz constitution of 1812, which, in turn, was very dependent on French constitutional experience. Since the Spanish and French constitutions have sections and clauses quite similar to the United States document, the Chilean constitutions have characteristics that are familiar to North Americans. The constitution of

1818 established a republic with a supreme director instead of a president, and a unicameral legislature, a senate of five members. It provided for the standard civil liberties of the age, those that are to be found in the United States, French, and Spanish constitutions. There was, as one would expect, strong emphasis on individual rights, especially property rights.

On the issue of slavery, Chileans were progressive for their era. An 1811 congressional action declared that in the future children born to slaves would be free. Slaves brought into Chile would be free after six months residence in the country. Slavery was fully abolished in 1823.

The concern about private property rights might have proved embarrassing to the government during the early years of the O'Higgins administration were the Chileans not rather pragmatic about ideology. O'Higgins became supreme director of Chile on February 16, 1817. Royalists controlled a good deal of Chilean territory, especially in the south, and there was practically no public treasury of which to speak. Consequently, three days after being appointed, O'Higgins decreed the confiscation of all royalist property. Later only the property of royalists who refused to reside within the country could be confiscated. Such property was a major source of public funds during the first years of the O'Higgins administration. When it came down to the fundamental issue of dollars and cents, the Chilean classical liberals could stretch a point.

Though the Chileans could be conveniently pragmatic when it came to the urgent need to raise public funds, they nevertheless wrote a distinctly liberal—though not democratic—constitution. This is evident in the nature of the senate. Its central responsibility was to insure observance of the organic code. It was given the broad and effective powers that a legislature should possess in a republican form of government. Senate approval was required on all important matters, such as "imposing taxes, soliciting loans, declaring war, making peace, forming treaties of alliance, commerce, neutrality; sending ambassadors, consuls, deputies or envoys to foreign powers; raising new troops or sending them outside the State; undertaking public works and creating new authorities or employs." The senators could overrule the supreme director's veto. This provisional document, which lasted some 5 years, permitted the supreme director to appoint the 5 senators. Even so, the senate proved to be independent and the backbone of Chilean liberalism. The character of both the senate and the Chilean political system can be seen in the relations between the senate and supreme director. Several examples will highlight the essence of this relationship. In December 1819 San Martín, the hero of Chilean independence, had requested 280,000 pesos from the Chilean government to mobilize the *Expedición Libertadora* to Peru. The senate refused to concede the sum, indicating that the treasury already had made sizable contributions to the venture and could not afford further financial burdens. The statement was not couched in diplomatic terms; no effort was made to suggest that the treasury would be able to afford such expenditures in the future. This unexpected action provoked San Martín into a pique that was not assuaged even when the senate later approved a smaller sum. The supreme director did not suffer the senate's spontaneous autonomy alone. In January 1820 the supreme director presented a routine budget for naval stores, and the senate refused to accept it. Later O'Higgins proposed the creation of a corps of military engineers, and the senate refused to give its approval to the scheme due to the shortage of funds.

Two senatorial actions of 1819 are of special interest. During the previous year O'Higgins had decreed the abolition of the mayorazgos, the entailed estates, one of his most famous actions. In December 1819 the senate reversed O'Higgins's decree by postponing its authority "for now." The supreme director's attack on the landed aristocracy lost him more powerful friends than it gained him. Also in 1819 the senate made a bold foray into military matters. O'Higgins, a highly regarded general, was ordered to accelerate his efforts to ready the *Expedición Libertadora* for departure, whether or not San Martín and his Argentine troops were prepared to accompany it. The senate now was deciding how fast an army should be prepared for war. That the senators were disposed to undertake the conquest of Peru without

San Martín and his Argentine troops bespeaks the growing sense of national identity in Chile.

In 1820 the senate attempted to supervise San Martín's activities in Peru, much to O'Higgins's anguish. In the spring of the year the senate was informed that royalists were becoming dangerously active in the province of Concepción. O'Higgins was therefore authorized to send troops and matériel by land and sea to the south. Chile was now fighting a war at home and one abroad. At this juncture the supreme director proposed salary increases for certain military officers. The senate refused to approve the raises. O'Higgins certainly was something less than an absolute dictator. In December the senate abrogated all wartime extraordinary powers that had been granted to the supreme director.

So truculent was the senate that in 1821 O'Higgins even thought of dissolving it. At a time when he needed funds to prosecute the war in Peru and fight guerrilla bands in the south of Chile, the senate lowered import duties on selected items and terminated a special monthly tax contribution. O'Higgins wrote to San Martín that he was faced with the choice of dissolving the senate or losing the province of Concepción. This was the man who had abolished titles of nobility and besieged the landed aristocracy and the church. His progressivism was now being strained beyond its limits. If his own personally appointed senators were acting so contrarily, "what will those who are indifferent and elected by the unbridled multitude do?"

In January of the following year, 1822, O'Higgins made one of his most serious political blunders; he attempted to dissolve the senate. Because of other obligations not all senators were available for sessions. One was sent to Rome to meet with Vatican officials and another to Peru as the Chilean representative to the new government. A third of the five desired to return to private life. With only three or possibly two senators left O'Higgins suggested that the senate temporarily suspend sessions and transfer its duties to the supreme director.

O'Higgins had directly challenged the very essence of Chilean constitutionalism. The senate responded by declaring that it considered itself unauthorized to suspend its sessions or transfer its authority to the supreme director. Without the senate, the senators argued, there would be no constitution. If there were no longer a need for the senate then a congress should be convened to which it would turn over its powers. Historian Diego Barros Arana claims that the senate itself had suggested it suspend sessions the previous year. Even if this were so the circumstance in 1821 was critically different. For one thing, it would have been the senators themselves proposing the suspension. Also the wartime situation was more threatening then. But perhaps most importantly, by 1822 Minister Rodríguez Aldea had become the most powerful figure in the administration after O'Higgins, and in many respects he was running the government. Each month he was becoming more powerful and less popular. It may very well have been because of him that the senators were concerned about their role in the Chilean constitutional system.

In any event it is certain that independent Chile's first legislature was highly emancipated, and although its logic may not always have been perfectly untarnished and impeccable, it early set itself up as the guardian of the Chilean constitutional system and a counterpoise to executive authority. Later legislatures would do the same.

Chile's next constitution was promulgated in 1822. Like its predecessor it judiciously guaranteed individual freedoms. A three-branch republican government was created, with a bicameral congress in which the chamber of deputies was the more powerful. A cabinet was provided for, the composition of which amply demonstrates how notably eclectic the Chilean constitution makers were. The cabinet was composed of ministers, and the supreme director was not given the privilege of appointing all of them. All bishops were ministers, and each university was required to name its own minister to the cabinet. The Chileans took the concept of balanced powers seriously; their organic codes clearly did not give the supreme directors and later presidents overweening powers.

One of the reasons the constitution of 1822 endured only about a year is that its centralizing tendencies antagonized the provinces of Concepción and Coquimbo. In addition to the three provinces, the country was divided into departments, each governed by an official named by the supreme director. The provinces were disgruntled by this clause and the rebellion which shortly led to O'Higgins's resignation not surprisingly was led by Concepción and Coquimbo.

Prior to the constitution of 1833, which lasted for nearly a century, Chile had two more constitutions and a series of organic federalist laws. The succeeding constitution of 1823 was an extreme manifestation of the classically liberal doctrine. While on the one hand it lowered the voting age (to twenty-one if single or earlier if married), on the other it added property and employment requirements. It protected individual property rights and yet had a section called *Moralidad Nacional,* which in brief called for the formulation of a moral code to detail the responsibilities of the citizen at all levels of age and stages of his social life.

Chile's 1826 experiment with federalism was short-lived. It was followed by the controversial constitution of 1828. Compared to the doctrinaire document of 1823 it displayed a more progressive approach, but finally it was by modern standards unmistakably conservative. It established Roman Catholicism as the official religion of the state to the exclusion of the public worship of any other. It adopted the same age requirement for citizenship and the franchise as the constitution of 1823, but it also maintained property and employment requirements, although these were reduced. Article 10 was right out of the mainstream of Lockean classical liberalism: "The Nation assures each man, as inviolable and imprescriptible rights, *liberty, security, property, the right of petition, and freedom to publish his opinions."* (Italics in the original.) Article 17 stated specifically that no citizen could be deprived of his property. Yet Article 126 did indeed deprive citizens of their property.

It was, in fact, Article 126 more than any other that gave the constitution of 1828 a reputation for democratic tendencies. This article abolished the mayorazgo, the entailed estate. After asserting that there were no privileged classes, the article abolished the sinew that held the landed aristocracy in its exalted place. No longer could estates—the article specified landed estates—be passed along in major portion to a single heir. This article presents one of the mysteries of Chilean history. It is difficult to determine why the issue of mayorazgo was so important to the senate during the O'Higgins administration that it would overrule the supreme director when now the constitution makers were willing to alienate the few but powerful mayorazgos and other leading estate owners who might merely have desired to pass most or all of their property along to a single heir. A tentative answer is that with each year the landed aristocracy held less sway over the active Chilean citizenry. Estate owners surely controlled votes at the provincial and local level, but this does not mean that they controlled the attitudes of the members of the broad bourgeoisie who held public office and attended constitutional conventions. The issue of mayorazgo was less heated and less controversial in 1828 than it had been earlier. It was not the central characteristic of the constitution to most Chileans, and it was not the critical issue to those who sought to reform the constitution in 1831.

Chile's next constitution was promulgated in 1833 and was Spanish America's second longest-lived organic code. It was replaced by the constitution of 1925. An understanding of the constitution of 1833 and its origins is essential to an understanding of much of nineteenth-century Chilean history.

The man generally given credit for the new constitution and the political stability that would bring distinction to Chile during the remainder of the nineteenth century is Diego Portales. Portales was born in 1793, the son of one of colonial Chile's leading professional bureaucrats, José Santiago Portales, who was superintendent of the royal mint at Santiago during the last decade of the colonial period. Rather than the bureaucracy, his son chose a career in commerce.

Diego Portales went to Peru in 1821 to conduct the foreign end of his newly formed merchant business and remained about two years. There he gave an indication of his developing nationalism. In 1822 he wrote that Lima, the city that for centuries had really been Santiago's metropolis, was ugly, "without resources or means of comfort, unhealthy and infested with flies and under military jurisdiction." In the decade of the 1830s he would go to war with Peru and Bolivia to protect Chile's place in the Pacific. Now Portales was ready to purchase a wide variety of goods, "giving preference to foreign articles, because this populace longs for everything foreign and abhors its own." Such chiding might suggest that Portales would have favored a policy of protection to support local productivity in the face of foreign competition. Only a few months later—at a time when his business venture was faring poorly—Portales was disturbed by a Peruvian interest in raising import duties, which threatened to cut off the Chilean goods on which his business depended. This is typical of the liberal economics of the Chilean bourgeoisie: they were free traders only when free trade was convenient. There were few ideological free traders in Chile until late in the nineteenth century.

It was during his Peruvian period that Portales also gave us a clear insight into his political preferences. He thought that democracy was absurd "in countries like the American, full of vices and where the citizens lack all virtue, as is necessary in order to establish a true *Republic*." He was opposed to monarchy as well. What he wanted was a republic. "But do you know how I understand it for these countries?" Then in just two sentences he presented his personal political code, something to which he adhered for the rest of his life. "A strong Government, centralizing, whose men are true models of virtue and patriotism, and set the citizens on the road of order and virtues. When they have made themselves moral, the Government comes to be completely liberal, free and full of ideals, where all citizens take part."

Portales returned to Chile to set his economic affairs in order. When he arrived, there was already talk of servicing the country's newly acquired external debt by placing the unproductive tobacco monopoly, the estanco, in private hands. A contract was signed in 1824 between the government and Portales, Cea y Cía., which granted the company the tobacco monopoly. In return, the company was required to service the external debt.

The estanco contract was a disaster for all concerned. The

tobacco monopoly had been established first in 1753, at a time when the Crown was generally liberalizing the mercantile system, and was quite unpopular with Chileans. It survived after the initiation of self-government largely because its restrictions were not judiciously enforced. Portales found himself with a bad deal. His company lacked sufficient capital to run the monopoly properly. The monopoly proved immediately unpopular, and many people grew and sold tobacco clandestinely so that Portales would have needed a fair-sized private army to frustrate all the illegal competition. Without capital, facing unpopularity, and being undermined by illegal competition, it is hardly surprising that the monopolists could not service the foreign debt.

The estanco contract was signed in August 1824. By February of the following year there was already a motion in congress to terminate it. Now the contract was becoming a major political issue. The political coalition known as the *pipiolos* mounted a vigorous public anti-estanco program and actively encouraged contraband. To fight such activity the monopolists and their supporters evolved into their own coalition, known as the *estanqueros*. For the first time in Chilean history businessmen were forced to form their own political group, a premodern party, and campaign publicly for their interests.

The estanqueros were not only concerned about protecting their political flanks, they were concerned about securing a personally favorable liquidation of the estanco contract. In 1826 the contract was canceled by the government and a commission was created to carry out its liquidation. The estanqueros waged a private and public propaganda war to see to a favorable settlement. Two years later the commission ruled that the government owed Portales, Cea y Cía. over 87,000 pesos. It was an announcement that entirely pleased the estanqueros and scandalized a good many others. Ultimately, it confirmed political positions already taken. By the time the contract was finally settled the estanqueros had become the central force in a broader political coalition called the pelucones. By 1826 the half dozen or so political groupings of significance had largely joined one or the other of the two major coalitions—the pelucones and the pipiolos. The driving force of the pelucón coalition was the estanqueros.

Diego Portales was soon to be politically powerful beyond anything he might have imagined only a few years earlier. After the estanco contract failed, he bought a press in Valparaíso and with limited financial resources published a paper to defend the contract and fight the opposing political forces. He also started a new business. In early 1827 he advertised the opening of his new commercial house in Valparaíso. "Send me," he urged a friend in April 1827, "by the first safe traveller . . . 200 pesos in natural silver for my private expenses, since I am without means and do not want to ask it of anyone here." After the settlement of the estanco contract none of Portales's political activities ever directly helped his business ventures.

A major revolt occurred in Chile as a result of the national elections of 1829. When the fighting broke out, Portales was in Valparaíso starting yet another business. He was now very disturbed by the political situation that was threatening the "tranquility necessary for conducting a business." By the end of 1829 the pelucones held control of the government. A Congress of Plenipotentiaries convened in Santiago in February 1830 and elected government officials. By early April José Tomás Ovalle was provisional president, and Diego Portales was minister of interior and minister of war. On April 17 the final battle of the revolt, at Lircay, was fought and the pelucón government was secure.

During his first ministry, from April 6, 1830, to August 31, 1831, Portales was the virtual dictator of Chile. In these seventeen months he created an emphatically stable, professional civilian government. Taking its cue from Portales the government was nonpersonalist and relatively nonpaternalistic. There were indeed famous and awe-inspiring public officials, and there was patronage to be wielded, but overall bureaucratic allegiance was paid to the system of government and later to the constitution of 1833. Since the pelucón coalition remained in power for many decades, bureaucrats did not have to worry about a wholesale turning out of office at each presidential election.

Portales was determined to have a civilian government. Even before the battle of Lircay, as minister of war he dismissed from the army Generals Borgoño, Lastra, Calderón, and Las Heras. These were indeed powerful figures. After Lircay over 100 officers were dismissed, among them former President Pinto. General Freire, defeated at Lircay, was exiled to Peru. Yet, on the other hand, Portales established a military academy to insure the presence of a nonpolitical, highly professional army. As a counterpoise to the military he created the civic guard, an institution that had previously existed but which was now reinstituted with vigor.

Though it was to be a civilian government, it would have clear religious overtones. Portales brought the church back into government, restored its privileges, and counted on it to cultivate a loyal populace. Portales wanted public tranquility, an atmosphere in which he could return to private business. A professional military and a nonpersonalist government supported by the church seemed to him obligatory ingredients of that tranquility.

It is difficult to determine Portales's influence over pelucón economics since his ministers of treasury were highly competent in their own right. In July 1830 he replaced his first minister, Meneses, with Manuel Rengifo, his old estanquero ally. Rengifo retired from his position in 1835 and then took it again in 1841 at the start of President Bulnes's administration. Rengifo was dedicated to the balanced budget and financial stability. He was also concerned with Chile's image in the world economic community, and it was he who, during his second term, initiated the systematic servicing of the country's foreign debt. During his first ministry he sought and achieved reductions in the armed forces and the governmental bureaucracy. When Portales returned to the central government in 1835 his minister of treasury was Joaquín Tocornal, who continued and even intensified the Rengifo programs and approaches.

It was Manuel Rengifo who set the pattern for pelucón economics, and it was a pattern that entirely pleased Diego Portales. Both were merchant-politicians, both believed in fiscal stability, balanced budgets, and lean bureaucracies.

By early 1831 Portales had determined finally to return to

private life and repair his own disheartening financial position. But before he could do so he was elected vice president. He refused the post and resigned all others he held. The congress unanimously declined to accept his resignation of the vice presidency and Portales nominally kept the position until it was written out of existence by the constitution of 1833. He also kept his title of minister of war and marine, although the ministry was run by another official.

Portales returned to Valparaíso in 1831 armed with impressive titles, but he was not—as so often pictured—the power behind the pelucón government. Several times he attempted to influence the central government and each time he was rebuffed. For instance, he tried to block the appointment of Colonel José María de la Cruz to the rank of general. Cruz got the appointment. In 1832 he was in the process of establishing a mill to smelt metals and to make the mill effective he needed a nearby port. He requested that the government build one for him. A bill was passed allowing its construction, but Minister of Treasury Rengifo refused to build it and that ended the matter. Portales was clearly much less than omnipotent during his Valparaíso period.

Once in Valparaíso Portales turned his legendary energy to reestablishing himself as a businessman. He outfitted the schooner *Independencia* to transport metals from the province of Atacama to the smelters and made plans for the construction of his own smelter. Believing it absurd to maintain the title of minister while acting as a full-time businessman, he finally got the government to accept his resignation in 1832. Yet at the end of that year he accepted the governorship of Valparaíso, a post he held for only about six months. He had decided to become a farmer and retired to work the nearby lands he had recently purchased. Here is another of the innumerable examples in Chilean history of a merchant taking up the agrarian life. One would think that he ran his farm much as he would any business. In fact, at the moment he thought his best financial prospects lay in farming.

By the middle of 1835 the pelucón coalition was on the verge of breaking apart. President Prieto and Minister of Interior Tocornal pleaded with Portales to return to the administration and save the day. Portales returned in 1835 and became minister of interior and foreign relations and minister of war and marine. For the next two years, until his assassination in June 1837, Portales ran the government of Chile more or less like a dictator.

The two most famous events of the Portales period were the promulgation of the constitution of 1833 and the offensive war against the Peru-Bolivian Confederation, which Chile began at the end of 1836 and won in 1839. The war was strictly Portales's doing. He feared the power of the Confederation in the Pacific. To Manuel Blanco Encalada, soon to be his chief of military forces, Portales wrote: "The position of Chile in relation to the Peru-Bolivian Confederation is indefensible. It cannot be tolerated by the people nor by the Government, because this would be equivalent to suicide." United, these two states would outweigh Chile in all matters. Portales's insights into power politics were sharp and sophisticated. It was not so much the dictator of the Confederation, General Andrés Santa Cruz, whom he feared, but the Confederation "directed by a man less capable than Santa Cruz." Portales engaged in a diplomatic polemic initiated by Santa Cruz "only to win time and to arm ourselves." He realized, however, that this tactic served Santa Cruz as well as Chile. "It is, then, in our interests to end this advantage that we are giving the enemy." Portales rose to the occasion. It must be the Confederation's last hour. "We must dominate forever in the Pacific." Chile was seriously outnumbered in manpower, but Portales believed the national spirit of the Chilean soldiers would carry the day. Perhaps it was this that brought Chile its first—but not most profitable— victory in an international war. If nationalism contributes to nationhood, then Chile was a full-fledged nation by 1836.

Neither the pelucón administration nor Portales dictated the writing of the constitution of 1833. The administration itself was not united on a constitutional plan, and the government's own newspaper, the *Araucano,* publicly attacked the plan presented by Mariano Egaña, the man one would think most represented the views of Portales and the pelucón government.

A constitutional convention was called to reform the constitution of 1828, but it ended by vigorously rewriting it. The new document was infinitely more conservative than its predecessor. It established the traditional three branches, with a bicameral legislature and a president eligible for two five-year terms. Consequently, the first four presidents under the new code—Prieto, Bulnes, Montt, and Pérez—each served ten years. In 1871 a law was passed which made it impossible for presidents to serve successive terms. Although the president was given extensive power and was through legal and extralegal means able to control presidential elections, the congress was an equal partner in government and given abundant power also. The legislative branch had already asserted itself and established its central position in Chilean governments. The political system created by the new code did not endure so long because it gave power to the presidents alone, but because it balanced the government and created a strong congress.

Considering its conservative bent it is not surprising that the new constitution established high voting requirements. Single men could vote at twenty-five and married men at twenty-one. There was also a property and income requirement as well as a reading and writing qualification, although the latter was designed not to go into effect for seven years. And true to the tone of government so recently established by Diego Portales, the constitution granted special fueros, judicial privileges, to the church while denying them to the military.

Two features of the new constitution more than any others have led to its reputation as the special handiwork of a pelucón government dominated by a conservative landed aristocracy: the document abolished provincial assemblies and reinstated mayorazgos. The government did not write the constitution and the landed aristocracy—in the sense that it can be singled out—was not the dominant force in Chilean politics during the pelucón administrations. All three plans considered by the constitutional convention had elaborately provided for provincial assemblies. They were abolished at the behest of Manuel José Gandarillas, editor of the *Araucano,* the delegate who most vehemently fought to maintain the more advanced features of the constitution of 1828, the man who openly attacked Mariano Egaña's conspicuously conservative plan. The fact is that many of the more progressive of the pelucones, like Gandarillas, favored strong central governments and realized that provincial assemblies might be anything but progressive institutions at times.

The new constitution did not reinstate mayorazgos (they had been abolished by the 1828 code) because the landed aristocracy mounted a campaign in their favor. Not one of the three plans considered by the constitutional convention even mentioned the issue of mayorazgo. It was only during the debates that the matter was raised. Naturally, the large landowners would favor entailed estates, but so, too, did many businessmen. They were more concerned about the establishment of a stable government than reforming the landholding system. In September 1832 the *Mercurio* of Valparaíso, the country's leading private newspaper and the voice of the country's most important commercial center, urged the constitutional convention to consider the consequences of abolishing the mayorazgo. The editors considered it impolitic to abolish at the present time such rights as the mayorazgos, and the military and ecclesiastic fueros. "After a solid government has been obtained," the editors observed, "then the Government can sanction a law that terminates one or the other, something that can be done without risk of threatening the tranquility of the State." Only the military fuero was abolished by the new constitution. The pelucón government was permitted to establish its stability without the alienation of the large landowners and the church. It had already reduced the military to manageable proportions.

The mayorazgo was not abolished finally until the 1850s, at which time it was defended more vigorously by the business community than the few mayorazgos. In June 1850 the *Mercurio* of Valparaíso wrote:

> The cause of order, the cause of liberty, the cause of equality, the cause of agriculture, of commerce, of industry, of public utility, in a word, the cause of right, of law and of justice, the cause of the dignity of public men, all clamour for the sincere and loyal interpretation of article 162 of the Constitution of 1833.

The Valparaíso business community had much to lose by a reinterpretation of the property rights clauses in the constitution. So robust and dynamic had the bourgeoisie become by the middle of the nineteenth century, however, that merely the possession of an aristocratic name was no longer enough to many of the children of the landed rich. Now they also wanted a piece of the action, now they also opposed the entailment of estates and their exclusion from the riches.

With the promulgation of the constitution of 1833 the Chilean political system was firmly established. It was a liberal system, in the nineteenth-century sense of the term, and it was designed in part to prevent the rise of popular democracy. It was the fruit of a bourgeoisie that was very much a part of the Western bourgeois tradition. It catered to the landed aristocracy but was neither created by it alone nor subservient to it.

5

THE PROBLEMS OF INDEPENDENT NATIONHOOD

At the time of independence Chile was troubled by fewer serious problems than most other Spanish-American nations. The society was relatively stable, at least when compared to countries like Mexico. The "white" population that dominated society was fairly homogeneous. Beneath it in the hierarchy stood the large group of *mestizos,* those of mixed European and Indian blood, who adapted themselves—some more successfully than others—to the Western way of life. Beneath the mestizos were the few Indians who did not reside in the far south. Most of the Indians lived segregated in the south and, therefore, did not create the social problems that vitiated stability in many other countries. And also unlike some of the other countries in newly independent Spanish America, Chile had few blacks and perhaps only 20,000 or 25,000 thousand people with noticeably Negroid features. This ingredient for potential racial tension, therefore, did not exist. Nor was land a problem. There was more than enough for anyone who desired it, except the very poor. The church did not become a problem because it owned little land in a country where land was plentiful and because it was quickly granted its special privileges and status and incorporated into the state. Chile did not possess the immense and geographically unmanageable territory that many of the other new countries did. This contributed to both a homogeneity and an early sense of national identity. The tradition of praetorianism activated during the wars of independence and so destructive to many Spanish-American countries did not take root in Chile. The Chilean military was quickly civilianized and professionalized. It has been the least politicized of the Spanish-American militaries and did not mount a *coup* on its own behalf until well into the twentieth century. Finally, Chile did not suffer from the lack of qualified personnel to form its bureaucracy. There were enough competent and professional bureaucrats in Chile in 1810 to form the basis of an expanded professional bureaucracy in the early nineteenth century. After independence was declared Chile wisely welcomed royalists and even foreigners. Thus José Antonio Rodríguez, a royalist, and Andrés Bello, a foreigner, became important members of the bureaucracy. The Chileans had some trouble figuring out how to run a congress, and it took time and effort to decide what parts of the complex body of colonial royal legislation should be applicable to the new country, but there was a professional and competent bureaucracy to get the new state over the rough spots.

There were, however, two major problems—federalism and neocolonialism. The spirit of regionalism, the desire of the provinces not to be dominated by Santiago, caused grave instability during the early national period. There were clear colonial origins to the federalist movement, and they were both economic and political. For instance, in 1794 the town of Concepción held a cabildo abierto for the purpose of fighting a special tax that the audiencia wanted extended. To redress Chile's negative trade balance with Peru a five-year tax on exports to that region had been established. (This may seem counterproductive now, but it was a means of raising money for the colonial government to balance its budget.) The southerners argued that the tax was illegal because it had been established without a hearing from the municipal attornies, a colonial right. They were opposed to taxation without representation and to actions of the central government that unfairly favored the economic interests of the Santiago-Valparaíso axis. The southerners lost their case and were harshly reprimanded.

During the early national period the provinces, especially Concepción, defended their interests keenly and were quick to call out their militia to back their demands. The south stood up to Carrera and then led the rebellion that caused O'Higgins's resignation. Southern rebellions were famous even at the middle of the nineteenth century.

Sometimes the regional spirit served the nation by keeping the central region honest and on its toes, but at other times the spirit of regionalism threatened progress. For instance, when the contract for a Santiago-Valparaíso railroad was being discussed in 1847, Senator Meneses, who held a doctorate in canon law, was a royalist during the independence movement and rector of the National Institute during the late 1820s, argued against the contract because by "bettering so much the transportation of the produce of the province of Santiago, the produce of the other provinces will be prejudiced in such a manner that they will not value much in the market." Meneses's argument was effectively torn apart by Minister of Interior Vial. Two years later Concepción's *Correo Del Sur* argued against the steamship monopoly enjoyed by the Pacific Steam Navigation Company on the grounds that it was the "convenience of Valparaíso and the towns of the North." The paper asserted that the steam monopoly was "pernicious because the southern provinces gain nothing by it, and because it is necessary to attend the general good of the country and not several areas in particular." Here the south's sense of its own needs and its willingness to speak up for them proved a valuable corrective tonic; the south was not receiving its fair share of the steamship service provided the country under the monopoly. The monopoly was, in fact, terminated.

The other of Chile's major problems during the early national period was neocolonialism. Chile was a preindustrial capitalist country in 1810, one that had been reared under the protection and tutelage of mercantilism and one that with independence was thrust into the world capitalist market strictly on its own. The young country sorely needed money and arms to prosecute the independence effort, and it needed more merchants and ships than it possessed. Later it needed more capital for its internal improvements schemes than Chileans were willing to provide. All this left Chile somewhat dependent on foreigners. Since it also desired recognition from at least one important foreign power (recognition from either the United States or Great Britain would have been sufficient to insure the country's independence), Chile had to court the countries from which the foreigners came.

Once the national junta was established in September 1810, Chile offered foreigners excellent trading possibilities. The new national government considered it mandatory to develop its defenses against potential aggression. To do this it needed arms. In early November a contract was celebrated with the British merchant Diego Whitaker, who agreed to bring to Chile among other articles 10,000 rifles, 10,000 pairs of pistols, and 2,000 sabers. Whitaker does not seem to have complied with the contract. With such needs, however, there is little likelihood that the new government would go out of its way to alienate the foreign merchants doing business in Chile, merchants who could secure matériel. But there is another side to the arms picture. The government understood that without the approval of such countries as Great Britain and the United States the task of importing war matériel would become further complicated. (Still in November a commission approved a plan of defense drawn by Juan Mackenna which called for the raising of a militia of 25,000 troops and the addition of 25,000 rifles to the existing supply. For the immediate future he wanted the purchase of 12,000 rifles, 12,000 swords, 5,000 pistols, and 25,000 lances.) Since the major European threat was considered to be Napoleon, since Spain was not in a position to supply arms, and since the viceroy of Peru was thought by some to be an active threat to the junta's integrity, the English-speaking merchants were in an enviable position to do business.

All this was made evident in the famous free trade decree of February 21, 1811. The decree opened the ports of Valdivia, Talcahuano, Valparaíso, and Coquimbo to traffic from "foreign powers, friends and allies of Spain and also of neutrals." Foreigners were prohibited from trading at any other points along the coast, although some of them long managed to do so by claiming the need of an emergency stop. The foreign merchants who obeyed the law could sell their cargos only at the four stipulated ports or the capital cities of the provinces in which the ports were located. The most serious restriction was that foreigners were not permitted to participate in the retail trade; they were limited to the wholesale trade.

It was under the aegis of this trade decree that the foreign merchant community slowly began to increase its ranks. The most important two groups were the British and North Americans. There is no indication that the Chilean government favored either group: it wanted arms and considered both the United States and Great Britain likely sources. Thus, for instance, in the early months after the proclamation of freedom of trade Valparaíso governor Juan Mackenna made informal arrangements with two United States commercial captains and one from Great Britain to encourage traffic in or to procure arms. The United States and Great Britain each had peculiar advantages for dominating trade in the new country. By 1812 the United States had both major and minor diplomats stationed in Chile, sometimes more than one of each. They acted officially to support the commercial needs of their compatriots. Great Britain did not have its first consul in Chile until 1824. But on the other hand, Great Britain enjoyed the advantages of available capital and manufactures. It also had special trade privileges with Brazil, something which facilitated its trade with the rest of the continent.

It was not until the establishment of the patriot government and the election of Bernardo O'Higgins to the supreme directorship in 1817 that the foreign merchant communities, especially the British, really began to prosper. The British were in an especially favorable position. For one thing, they were already beginning to increase in numbers. For another, Supreme Director O'Higgins, whose father was Irish and who himself had lived and studied in England, was predisposed toward the British and their brand of liberalism. The question of recognition was also important. After independence was declared in 1818, the government made a concerted effort to win recognition from the foreign powers. Attention was centered on Great Britain. But perhaps the most consequential factor was the potential role of the British navy. In order to prosecute the war against the remaining royalists in the south and then later to patronize the liberation of Peru, which involved transporting the *Expedición Libertadora* by sea, O'Higgins well appreciated the desirability of keeping the British fleet in the Pacific friendly or at least neutral. But in light of these advantages the influence of the British merchants resident in Chile during the early national period was limited.

Foreigners prevailed because Chile wanted them there.[1] The chief source of income for the new government, other than property expropriation, was commerce, and to stimulate this it depended on the participation of foreigners. Although Chile possessed a relatively large and powerful merchant community during the late colonial period, this community was seriously dislocated during more than a decade and a half of war, including a period of exile for many leading merchants. Now that Chileans were able to export their products at will, their minute merchant marine was not sufficient to do the job and foreign ships were required. Also, the efforts and resources of many Chileans who might have gotten involved in commerce were still directed at the local war effort and the plans to liberate Peru. The Chileans required commerce, manufactures, and diplomatic recognition, and to get these they needed foreign merchants, both residents and transients.

Some Chileans were not troubled by the presence of foreigners while others were. For instance, in 1822 Diego Portales wrote this of United States recognition of the independence of Spanish America: "Beware of leaving one domination in order to fall into another!" He felt that the United States was following a preconceived plan for effecting "the conquest of America, not through arms, but through influence in all spheres. This will happen, perhaps today no; but tomorrow yes." But Portales was not influential at the time and his opinions were not shared by all. Hence José de Irisarri, formerly interim supreme director and soon to be minister plenipotentiary in Europe, advised O'Higgins in

---

[1] British traveler Samuel Haigh visited Valparaíso in 1817 and 1828. He states that there were 2 English residents there in 1817 and about 2,000 in 1828 (Samuel Haigh, *Sketches of Buenos Ayres and Chile* [London, 1829], p. 176). However, British industrialist John Miers thought that during the O'Higgins period Valparaíso did not have more than "four hundred Englishmen," including transients. (John Miers, *Travels in Chile and La Plata*, 2 vols. [London, 1826], Vol. I, p. 446.)

1817 of the advantages of an intense European migration to Chile. The future "Deputy of Chile in London," which he became, Irisarri informed the supreme director, "ought to work incessantly in promoting the emigration of industrious men, manufacturers, mechanics, chemists and other useful people who are perishing in France, England, and other European nations." Irisarri was rather pessimistic about the course the Spanish-American independence movement was taking. The active support of one of the major European powers or recognition from one might be the decisive factor in guaranteeing success. After all, he noted, seven years have gone by since the start of the independence movement and "still we are like the first day, neither more nor less." And "while our luck is not assured in any way, our commerce cannot gather much momentum." Irisarri proposed a solution to both problems: "Suppose that it were necessary to offer to England, or to France ten years of exclusive trade with us in return for their decision in our favor? What would it be that we would lose in this?" As one might suspect, Irisarri is remembered as one of the more controversial figures of the Spanish-American independence movement. He would go further than an exclusive privilege; he suggested ceding England one of Chile's southern islands. "What evil would come to us from having for neighbors and for friends the English?" Such a plan was actually written into Irisarri's 1818 ministerial instructions, which, however, were never signed by O'Higgins. With government officials in this frame of mind it is no wonder that foreign merchants, especially the British and North Americans, would consider Chile a likely place to set up shop.

There is no indication that the foreign merchants were competing against each other by nationality except insofar as foreigners from the same country tend to socialize and do business with each other. For instance, there is no evidence that foreign national groups sought commercial advantages during the O'Higgins period to the exclusion of other foreign national groups. The government seems to have treated each solicitation for privilege merely on the basis of its merit and the degree to which it would benefit the country. Thus in 1818 the government decreed that Jorge Cood, "natural de Lóndres," could take part in the nation's mining industry with the same privileges enjoyed by native Chileans. But the decree added that this grant also applied to "the foreigners from whatever other nation who want to take part in such an important labor."

The year 1818 offers a vivid example of the problems confronting the new country as it competed in the world capitalist market. By the middle of the year the government had won what appeared to be its terminal battle with the remaining royalists in the south, declared its independence, and launched a naval war against the Spanish fleet. During the year the foreign merchant community actually became its partner in a business venture. In March the British merchant ship *Windham* docked at Valparaíso and was sold to the government for 180,000 pesos, 25,000 pesos of which were contributed by several merchants in return for participation in prize money. The ship was outfitted for war and became the famous *Lautaro*. So successful was it that in June the foreign partners were paid off in full. The problem for Chile in 1818 was not a choice between capitalism and socialism, for this choice did not exist, but a choice between war and colonial status. Had Chile entered the world capitalist system in a state of peace, the *Windham* could have become a key factor in a merchant marine that could have lessened the country's dependence on foreign merchants.

During the remaining years of the O'Higgins tenure the government continued granting privileges to foreigners based on its need and their merit. British merchants were not the only ones showing initiative. Two North Americans, Jeremy Robinson and Charles Wooster, were granted important exclusive business privileges, though each received his for fewer years than he had requested. A Chilean, Agustín Eyzaguirre, organized a company to trade with India. British ships had been arriving in Chile with consumer goods from Europe, selling them at Valparaíso, picking up copper, gold, and silver, and then proceeding to Asia. There they took on Asian goods such as tea and spices and sailed back to Europe. Now the Chileans wanted a part of this lucrative trade. The government granted their first ship, the *Carmen,* the right of duty-free export and a 6,000-peso import reduction for the first trip. However, though a trade was started, the Eyzaguirre operation did not endure long.

It was in this atmosphere that British merchant Carlos Higginson requested permission to enter the nation's coastal trade—the *cabotaje*. The captain and owner of the British brigantine *Tiber* had recently joined the Chilean navy to serve as an officer on the *Lautaro*. While he was "contributing with his services to the triumph of the independence of Chile," he left his ship in care of Higginson in the hope that it be used in the cabotaje. Even under such mitigating patriotic circumstances the government remained adamant concerning the nation's coastal trade. Higginson's petition was rejected, probably because the government thought that Higginson intended to operate the ship himself. The ship, however, could be used if it were in the employ of Chilean nationals. It was in part because of the advantages of participating in the cabotaje that many foreigners were now requesting citizenship.

Though the Chilean government desired to assert its independence and integrity, the wartime situation made this difficult. In December 1819, following the advice of both the senate and merchant tribunal, it decreed that no foreigner could participate in the cabotaje or retail trade without first obtaining Chilean citizenship. Yet the exigencies of the war effort—the expeditionary force was being prepared, a fleet was operating in the Pacific, and there was a resurgence of royalist activity in the south—placed the government in a precarious position. It wanted to limit the activities of the foreigners and yet was dependent on them for the war effort. Thus, when two Chilean merchants, Francisco Ramón de Vicuña and José Joaquín Larraín, attempted to win a government contract to carry provisions to the troops in the south, they were turned down. Minister Echeverría wrote to the governor of Valparaíso that, "For now it is suitable that the provisions go in foreign ships in order to cut the risks and delays." And it should be noted that these two Chileans came from prestigious and powerful families. Yet the government had trouble finding foreign ships interested in such work, and it was soon suggesting to the governor that a national ship should be used if there were any delays.

The degree to which foreigners had become influential in Chile during the O'Higgins period can be demonstrated by the extent to which the government allowed them religious privileges. Not only did O'Higgins desire immigrants from Protestant countries and appreciate the benign effect a liberal policy would have on their governments in reference to recognition, but he was also a religious liberal, one who had taken severe measures against the church. At the end of November 1819 a group of Protestants wrote to O'Higgins requesting permission to purchase land in the environs of Santiago and Valparaíso to bury their dead. Since only Catholics could be buried in Chile, Protestants sometimes converted on their deathbeds simply to insure burial. Perhaps the most interesting feature of the letter O'Higgins received is that the first signature was that of W. H. Shirref, commander of the British fleet in the Pacific. It would become typical in the future for the British community to turn to its leading naval officer in the region to support its appeals to the government. The North Americans had diplomats and the British had the fleet. (Not all the letter signers were British.) In addition to his own views on religion and immigration, the supreme director could not have been anxious to estrange the British fleet just as he was hoping the *Expedición Libertadora* would sail for Peru. In December he granted the Protestants the license they solicited and permission to bury their dead according to the rites of their own religion.

The British community soon had to invoke the powers of their fleet once again. Early in 1820 the government deemed it necessary to raise 300,000 pesos to conclude the final preparations for the *Expedición Libertadora*. In March the senate decided that it would be useless to impose an additional forced contribution on the monasteries and clergy, who, it concluded, had little left to give. During the previous year it had noted that the commercial community hardly contributed to the war effort, largely because it was comprised mainly of foreigners who were not subject to the forced loans. Now it ruled that foreigners with Chilean citizenship must contribute their quota of the 300,000 pesos, and all other European foreigners were requested to make "some voluntary loan in order to aid our cause." The government, too, found a collateral financial advantage to citizenship.

The British soon objected. Great Britain had recently declared itself neutral in the Spanish-American wars for independence, and now the British subjects appealed to the commander of the British naval forces in the Pacific to guarantee them as neutrals protection against the senate's order that they pay taxes. The commander supported their claim. Soon the senate declared that "the complaint of the English merchants . . . absolutely lacks in legal fundamentals." But in the name of harmony it suspended its previous ruling. This was July 6, and, though the *Expedición Libertadora* did not depart for over a month, it was expected that it would set sail before that late date. The neutrality of the British fleet in the imminent war of liberation loomed large in Chile's plans. Not before and never again did any resident foreign community successfully exert quite so much pressure on the O'Higgins administration. But this pressure should be considered in the perspective of Chile's wartime obligations.

An 1820 incident is highly instructive for an understanding of the problems Chile faced at its initiation as an independent state in the world capitalist system. The town council of the northern mining town of Huasco petitioned the government to permit foreigners to transport copper out of the mining provinces and to bring in provisions and trade items. The economy of the region was suffering, it argued, because the facilities of Chilean citizens to service it were insufficient. In April the senate declared that the cabotaje was reserved to citizens for the benefit of the nation. When they do not take advantage of the privilege and the miners suffer, then the regulations must be changed. O'Higgins supported the senate and decreed that while the citizens of the country continued to enjoy the exclusive privilege of coastal trade, foreigners could transport copper from the ports of Huasco and Copiapó. And if the citizenry could not satisfy the general trade requirements of the region, the foreigners could be licensed to fill the gap.

This was rather a daring step for the government to take, especially since several Chilean citizens had already voiced their disapproval of any such legislation. In March five Chilean citizens addressed a letter to the administration lucidly arguing their case. They pointed out that in exchange for lower shipping costs the miners would be forcing many Chileans out of work. They deplored the fact that the Chilean navy was comprised of many foreign sailors and even controlled by foreigners. This was all the more reason to develop a merchant marine. Another sore point was that the national ships carried all sorts of goods while the foreigners concentrated on the minerals, and thus this gainful trade fell under their control.

It is clear that Chileans were not united in their attitude toward the foreign merchants. But the most interesting aspect of the letter perhaps is that one of the five letter signers was Charles W. Wooster from the United States and another was Andres Blest from Great Britain. The foreign merchant communities were no longer monolithic. Now the question of citizenship divided the foreigners in such a way that it becomes quite impossible to determine the precise nature of their influence after 1820. They can no longer be considered one group.

There are two important lessons in the Huasco incident. One is that the Chilean government could easily have protected the local merchant marine had it chosen to do so. In the area of trade the Chileans had already adopted a rather non–laissez faire brand of capitalism. The other lesson is that many of the leading "foreigners" were, in any meaningful sense of the term, Chileans. They became Chilean citizens, often married Chileans, raised Chilean families, and lived the rest of their lives in their adopted country. Quite a few of the large so-called foreign merchant houses in Chile at mid-nineteenth century were foreign in name only; they were really Chilean merchant houses. It is true that some foreign merchants, like Wheelwright and Hill, made their fortunes and left the country, but many, like Edwards, Blest, Bunster, and Waddington, stayed. When speaking of these powerful merchants one cannot employ the term "neocolonialism."

During the early decades after the establishment of the 1810 junta many foreign merchants made fortunes in Chile. Some of the most important families in twentieth-century Chile were founded at about this time. One of the merchants, Joshua Waddington, became a philanthropist and, in the early 1850s, minister of treasury. In succeeding decades many of the foreign or foreign-Chilean merchant houses turned to banking and actively supported other sectors of the economy. But not all the foreigners were successful. Some, like John Miers, invested their fortunes and lost them. One of the problems facing people like Miers was that provincial officials were not always as eager to court the foreigners as those in the central government. Miers invested, according to his own account, about $80,000 in a venture to refine and finish copper. But, between the problems he faced dealing with provincial officials and the ill effects of an earthquake, Miers decided to give up and migrate to Argentina. As he tells it, the fates of the merchants Henderson and Wooster were similar to his own.

By the time the O'Higgins administration fell in early 1823 there was an important foreign merchant group resident in Chile. The source of the influence enjoyed by these merchants was not merely economic. Other factors, such as the presence of the British fleet and the question of recognition, were of equal and at times greater importance. Except in one instance the merchants do not appear to have taken advantage of these factors. They thrived because the government desired them to do so. They were not political activists: their goals, except for those relating to religion, closely reflected their economic needs and were hardly presumptuous. The government did not allow any foreign group economic privileges not available to other foreign groups. The government was never, not even during the taxation episode, obsequious to the British or any other foreign community.

During the period of political confusion that followed the fall of O'Higgins and endured until the pelucones took power, it is quite likely that the foreign merchants exerted a good deal of influence. But if this is so the situation must have altered markedly with the rise of Diego Portales to power. We already know that Portales was a great nationalist. In 1831 he wrote to one of his diplomats in France, "There is no reason at all for the foreigners resident among us to enjoy a better status than Chilean citizens." If the foreigners did not find Chilean justice adequate for their demands, he asserted, they had the alternative of leaving the country.

At about the same time, a British subject died in Valparaíso without leaving a will and the British chargé d'affaires requested that the deceased's personal property be turned over to him so that it could be forwarded to the next of kin. Portales replied that according to a decree of 1813 the Chilean government is empowered to do exactly that when a will has not been found if the country of the deceased has made similar provisions for Chilean nationals. Should the chargé present evidence that such was the case in Great Britain, the request would be taken care of without difficulty. The evidence presented by the chargé was unsatisfactory. A treaty between Britain and Spain signed in 1667 did cover Chileans, but as Spanish citizens. Portales reproved the chargé, reminding him that he could not "less than perceive that the interpretation of the Treaty is injurious to the rights of Chile as an independent and sovereign Nation."

As governor of Valparaíso Portales maintained a similar attitude. Late in 1832 Captain Paddock of the North American ship *Catherine* was refused a loan by the firm of Alsop y Cía. The captain responded by killing two employees of the firm. Running wildly through the streets of the port, he managed to kill or wound others also. Paddock was tried, convicted of murder, and sentenced to death. The national court of appeals confirmed the verdict. Many people intervened in an attempt to lessen the sentence, and it was quite generally believed in Valparaíso that Paddock had been temporarily deranged. The death penalty seemed inappropriate. United States diplomatic officials tried to persuade Portales to commute the sentence. In answer to a plea presented by members of the British community, Portales wrote, "I am naturally compassionate; but I am more a lover of the law, of good order and of the honor of my poor and unfortunate country." Captain Paddock was hanged.

Though Portales was a vigorous nationalist, and Chilean nationalism would soon lead the young country into an aggressive and successful war, Chile was still dependent on foreigners for its economic development during the pelucón administrations. This is most clearly evident in the business activities of William Wheelwright of Newburyport, Massachusetts.

Wheelwright's most spectacular early success was the establishment of the Pacific Steam Navigation Company, the PSNC, and the introduction of steam navigation to Chile and Pacific South America. As many Chileans understood, successful navigation of the Pacific waters was a national necessity. With the nineteenth-century transportation revolution it became quite clear that sail power left a good deal to be desired. The trip by sail from New York to Valparaíso generally took at least three months. The time it took correspondence to reach the United States or Europe was always long, sometimes scandalous. "No scheme can possibly be devised so effectually to correct these evils," Wheelwright wrote, "and to bring about a better order of things, as the establishment of a close and constant communication by steam; which is more essential from the almost total absence by sea." Wheelwright later found that sail power was also becoming unprofitable. During the early years of his steam venture he purchased a schooner to work between Callao and Panama, since his steamers traveled only as far as Callao. The first report of the PSNC noted that the schooner had been running at a loss and was therefore sold. "Experience has proved," the report stated, "that owing to calms and currents, sailing vessels cannot efficiently and profitably keep up a communication along that part of the coast."

The initial introduction of steam navigation to Chile occurred long before Wheelwright became interested in the project. In 1821 a United States citizen, Daniel S. Grisnold, presented the O'Higgins administration a solicitation requesting a concession of a fifteen-year exclusive privilege for the establishment of steam navigation in Chilean waters. He proposed to cut the fifteen-day trip from Concepción to Coquimbo down to between forty-five and fifty-eight hours. O'Higgins and his chief minister, Ignacio Zenteno, warmly received the solicitation and passed it along to the fiscal of the supreme court, who soon presented a negative opinion. The fiscal's conclusion was founded on three considerations. For one, the concession would conflict with a law which reserved the cabotaje for nationals. Second, he felt that steam navigation would lessen the need for sailors and consequently threaten the further development of a national merchant marine. Finally, he thought such a means of transportation would increase contraband activity.

O'Higgins demurred and sent the solicitation to an advisory tribunal which in turn passed it on to a two-member commission that approved it. In March 1821 the supreme director signed a decree which created Grisnold's concession. It showed that the fiscal's criticism had not gone totally unheeded. The foreigner was conceded a ten-year exclusive privilege to operate a steam vessel of 750 tons in Chilean waters under a Chilean flag. One quarter of the crew had to be Chilean. For some reason the franchise was never implemented.

This is an excellent example of the dilemma facing the young capitalist country. It had to give out an exclusive privilege, create a fiction about coastal trading, the cabotaje, and threaten the development of its own merchant marine just to secure an important internal improvement. The reason the government itself did not undertake this improvement is that it still functioned under the mercantilist concept of a balanced budget. The O'Higgins government was at war and hardly had the resources to pursue such a venture. The reason private Chilean citizens did not undertake it is that their physical and financial energies were turned elsewhere.

The next year a steam vessel did ply Chilean waters. The most famous sailor of the independence epoch, Lord Cochrane, had a steamship sent to him from England in 1822. Another steamer was brought to Chile in the same year. One seems to have gotten lost, and the other blew up. In any event, Wheelwright was the next person to attempt steam navigation in Chile.

In 1835 Wheelwright was granted a ten-year exclusive privilege "to establish the navigation of steam vessels in our ports and rivers open to coastal commerce, with the exemptions and known privileges, or those that will be conceded in the future to national shippers." Thus nationals lost their special position in coastal trading. If after four years steam navigation had not been established in one or more rivers, the privilege with respect to rivers would be terminated. This last was a senatorial attempt to insure that the country would receive at least minimal benefits from the steam monopoly.

Wheelwright, still a novice entrepreneur, had only 2 years in which to implement the franchise by placing 2 steam vessels in Chilean waters. He had trouble raising capital in both the United States and Great Britain and extensions had to be granted by the Chilean government. However, a board of directors was formed in London in 1838 for the PSNC, capitalized at £250,000, with 5,000 shares of stock offered at £50 each. A thousand shares were reserved for sale in South America. (Between 1830 and 1855 the Chilean peso was approximately equal to one-fifth of the British pound and approximately equal to the United States dollar.) After a whole catalogue of further problems, Wheelwright's 2 steamers, the *Chile* and the *Peru,* arrived in Chile during the southern winter of 1840. They were both 700 rather than the minimum 300 tons Wheelwright had promised the Chilean government.

Chile had its regular steam service only about two years after Cunard established his regular steam service between Britain and the United States. During the transportation and internal improvements revolution of the nineteenth century there was little or no technological lag between Chile and the rest of the Western world. Wheelwright solicited the government for a franchise for a telegraph company only six months after Morse made his spectacular demonstration of its feasibility in the United States. It took a while for the railroads to be built in Chile, but that delay was due to finances and not technological knowledge.

There is a memorable lesson about foreign economic colonialism in the PSNC venture. In 1844 the company announced that it had lost over £72,000 during its first four years of operation. Stocks had fallen to below £9 from their high of £40. But a contract to carry mail along the Pacific coast of South America was soon granted by the British government. The contract provided a fixed subsidy of £20,000 annually for 5 years. It was on the basis of this contract, a subsidy from the British government, that steam navigation functioned in Chilean waters during the remainder of the 1840s. With the mail contract the company began to gain its stride. In 1848 shareholders were greeted with their first dividend—2.5 percent!

The company was just getting on its feet when gold was discovered in California. The discovery profoundly affected the course of Chilean development at several levels. Initially, it triggered an exodus of ships and people, both sailors and gold seekers. Between December 1, 1848, and December 1, 1849, 303 ships left Valparaíso destined for San Francisco. Fifty-three were Chilean. California represented a new market of impressive dimension, but to partake of its great potential wealth, Chile needed ships, many more than were presently servicing the country.

To augment its sea facilities, the country had to modify its navigation laws. During the period 1834–1848, the Chilean government maintained a policy of open discrimination in favor of domestic shipping. National shipping interests were aided with special privileges and exemptions from various taxes and this in the face of opposition from powerful segments of the economy. Under the impact of the gold discovery this paternal legislation was totally dismantled in the ten years following 1848.

A navigation law of 1836 made it requisite that the captains, as well as the owners, of all national ships be Chilean. Three-quarters of the crew were to be Chilean. The law was given a twelve-year life period; it ended in 1848. Four months after the law became inoperable, the government decreed that foreigners could be proprietors of national ships. This was essentially official recognition of the prevalence of illegal procedure in registering ships under the Chilean flag. But this was not enough of a concession to the times. Foreign ships were not permitted to participate in the country's coastal trade, a privilege they wanted. As it became obvious that the supply line to California was a crucial factor in the nation's economic growth, the government began to act.

President Bulnes asked the congress, as it convened during the Chilean winter of 1849, to enable him to allow foreigners to participate in coastal trade for one year. The senate received the president's request first. Several of its influential members at once aligned themselves against the proposal. They were prompted by a fear that such privileges would emasculate the nation's own mer-

chant marine. Andrés Bello, one of Spanish America's most distinguished nineteenth-century scholars and then a Chilean senator,
argued against the president:

> until now one cannot say that we have a merchant marine truly
> Chilean; since in its major part it is of foreign ownership and con-
> struction. The Chilean marine, properly speaking, is nothing more
> than some masts with Chilean flags; I do not see anything else.
>
> In this sense, not only am I not disposed to approve the present
> project, but I would completely abolish all of these privileges. One
> of our most special interests is to protect the mineral industry and the
> exchange of the products of the northern provinces with those of the
> southern provinces. The merchant marine is the only agent that can
> carry these objects, and already because of such privileges we have
> not secured a merchant marine and it will be necessary to qualify
> foreign bottoms in order to obtain one.

Bello received the support of such leading statesmen as president
of the senate Benavente, but nonetheless the president's proposal
passed the senate and was sent to the chamber of deputies.

The deputies treated the measure to a wide range of arguments.
One of the more influential deputies was Bello's son Carlos, who
unlike his father was a leading advocate of free trade. (There are
several significant examples such as this in Chilean history that
serve to call into question the legendary political solidarity of the
famous Chilean and Spanish-American family groups. Members of
the same families neither always thought alike nor voted alike.)
Bulnes's proposal passed the chamber and became law in early
1851. It permitted foreigners to participate in the nation's coastal
trade for five years. The law also conceded the PSNC or any other
steam company the right to participate in coastal trade without
limitation of time.

The merchant marine was another of Chile's mid-nineteenth-
century problems. To prosper, the country had to move its products up and down its lengthy coast and export them, and to do this
it required a tremendously expanded merchant marine or foreign
participation. Many Chilean statesmen were classically liberal in
their political orientation and free trade (on a modified basis) was
entirely harmonious with their general views. It has been suggested
that allowing foreigners such privileges as participation in the

coastal trade was very consistent with the country's emphasis on development toward the outside, an emphasis rooted in Chile's basic lack of capital and its inability to compete industrially with the world metropolises.[2] The fact is, as shall be discussed in the following section dealing with rail development, Chile did not lack domestic capital at mid-century. The reason the country elected to develop toward the outside, as it is often put, would have been the same even if the country were Socialist at the time. Modified freedom of trade and socialism or planned economies in general are not necessarily incompatible.

The striking influence of the California gold discovery on the Chilean economy stimulated a positively optimistic atmosphere in 1849 and 1850. Wheelwright's ten-year exclusive privilege for steam navigation along the republic's coast was scheduled to expire in 1850, and amid the exuberance he was forced to solicit the government for an extension on the rights which he had originally won and were legally possessed by the PSNC. A petition was presented to the minister of interior a full year before the expiration date. In it Wheelwright rehearsed the general benefits of steam navigation to Chile and the hardships withstood by the company in the early years. But his appeal was not able to balance an upsurging nationalism and contend with the many successful businessmen now coveting a larger place in their country's economy.

At once provincial newspapers began attacking the monopoly. The northern and southern provinces clearly were not being properly serviced by the steam monopoly. The conservative paper *El Copiapino* editorialized in 1848 that it would be a disgrace for the country if the exclusive steam privilege continued. It is of absolute necessity, it suggested, that "we have one or two domestic steamers to service our littoral." Early in 1849 the paper suggested that a company be formed based on local capital. Gregorio Ossa Cerda, the noted northern capitalist, offered to put in 20,000 pesos. Immediate action was called for, but none was taken.

[2] The most famous exponent of this view is Andre Gunder Frank, *Capitalism and Underdevelopment in Latin America: Historical Studies of Chile and Brazil* (New York, 1969), pp. 4–6.

There was also an antimonopoly movement in the capital. Santiago's prestigious *Progreso* argued that the fundamental benefit of the steam monopoly, "to acclimatize steam in the Pacific," had already been given. "This benefit," the paper asserted, "has been paid for by 10 years of monopoly, and of tyranny, to which we resigned ourselves hoping things would become better. The true benefits of steam will come when the privilege has terminated." The editors were not worried that termination of the monopoly would threaten steam communication with Europe.

But others were indeed afraid of just such a possibility. The powerful *Mercurio* of Valparaíso favored an extension of the PSNC's exclusive privilege but with the provision that the company be required to extend its line to Chiloé and to provide periodic communication with California. A 5-year extended privilege would call for a 50,000-peso annual government subvention to the company. The paper concluded that without extension not only would the country not have, "North American steamers, not only will we not have steam communication with the provinces of the south, but we are in danger of losing steam communication with the provinces and towns of the North, and who knows but also with Europe later on."

President Bulnes supported Wheelwright's petition and a 50,000-peso annual subvention for a line to the south. He favored a subvention since the *privilege* to establish the southern line would not insure its accomplishment, as demonstrated by the present lack of service to as northerly a southern port as Talcahuano.

The chamber of deputies received Wheelwright's petition before the senate. Carlos Bello quickly set the tone for the discussion with a lucid argument opposed to an extension of the monopoly or a subvention. Bello was born in London in 1815 and arrived in Chile with his father in 1829. In 1840 he moved from Santiago to the Copiapó mining district and returned shortly with a fortune. From that point until his death in 1854 he was a deputy, poet, and novelist. After praising Wheelwright, he began ravaging the company, whose reputation, he believed, should not be confused with that of its founder. What advantages ought one enjoy from steam navigation? He answered:

> Celerity, convenience and punctuality.
> Celerity!—But a steamer takes twenty-four days from Panama to Valparaíso. This is from four to five miles per hour.
> And this excessive slowness is due to the steamers's short trips and inexcusable delays. Six or seven days in Callao, and meanwhile the important Valparaíso correspondence sleeps. And as a result an answer to a letter is received in Europe a month before one would be received in Lima traveling from Santiago or Valparaíso. Nevertheless, the distance that separates us can be managed in five or six days. I do not understand how Valparaíso has tolerated for so long such an unnecessary procrastination.

And for convenience, the crowding of "four passengers in a narrow cabin is a common sight." Speaking of the necessary line of communication with Europe, Bello argued that Great Britain would never relinquish its commercial advantage on the west coast of South America and would certainly see to it that a line was maintained. And California would not give up her granary, he asserted with great lack of insight. (In only a matter of years United States wheat undersold its Chilean competitor and effectively closed the California market to it.)

The chamber of deputies defeated Wheelwright's petition by nearly a unanimous vote. The PSNC no longer enjoyed a monopoly. Following the vote, it was noted that several nationals had solicited the government for rights to establish steam lines in the southern part of the country. Now that the steam monopoly had been defeated, the question of the subvention came to the floor and was approved. An annual subvention of 36,000 pesos for a period of 5 years was passed. Bello was an ardent supporter of the subvention.

Following a quick approval by the senate the minister of interior announced that bids would be accepted for the establishment of "the communication by Steam between Valparaíso and the south of the Republic to Chiloé." Bids were received from two parties and the subvention finally went to the company of Roberto Simpson and N. C. Ossa. The PSNC had not attempted to secure the subvention.

Carlos Bello must have been quite happy over the results. Without either the monopoly or a subvention the PSNC managed to provide its most frequent and efficient service to date. Nor was steam communication with the rest of South America or Europe terminated.

Altogether, the Chileans acquitted themselves very well against the British and North American steam colonialists.

Another of Wheelwright's ventures clarifies the issue of neo-colonialism. Wheelwright had thought seriously about the construction of railroads in Chile even before his steamship line was functioning. The need for a rail line connecting Santiago and Valparaíso was evident, and few living in the central region of the country had to be convinced of its desirability. The question was where the money would come from. Traditionally it was the empresario's responsibility to raise the capital at home or abroad. Chilean capitalists, as a rule, were not interested in investing in internal improvements. Roads and canals yielded relatively low interest rates, when, as the *Mercurio* of Valparaíso noted in 1833, ordinary business investments and personal loans yielded in the neighborhood of 18 percent.

This singularly critical point deserves widespread attention. Though some Chilean capital was being appropriated by the world capitalist metropolises, Chileans themselves had more than enough capital to finance all the important and vastly expensive internal improvements of the nineteenth century. Chileans had to rely on foreign capital for some of their internal improvements for two striking reasons. One is that Chileans preferred not to invest in low-interest-yielding ventures when they could earn several times more in traditional ventures. The second is that the country's tax structure and collection technique did not provide the central government with sufficient funds to meet the requirements of the nineteenth-century technological revolution. (These certainly are two limitations of capitalism and the nonplanned economy, but at mid-nineteenth century socialism was not yet an attractive alternative to those with effective franchise.)

In 1845 Wheelwright petitioned the government for a contract to construct the rail line between the capital and Valparaíso. He requested a 100-year exclusive privilege and a 5 percent guaranteed income on capital invested. There were many other requests, but these were probably the 2 most aggressive ones.

The two leading newspapers of the day, the *Mercurio* of Valparaíso and the *Progreso* of Santiago, immediately commenced a barrage of editorial analysis. Founded in 1842, the *Progreso* was Santiago's first daily newspaper. Domingo F. Sarmiento, later to be president of Argentina, was the first editor, serving from November 1842 to May 1843 and then again from March 1844 to October 1845. In 1849, Bartolomé Mitre, another Argentine exile destined for that country's presidency, became editor. The paper favored both the 100-year exclusive privilege and the 5 percent guarantee.

Founded in 1827 by Ignacio Silva Medina, a Chilean, and Thomas Wells, a North American, the *Mercurio* was consistently in the forefront of current events with its dedicated news coverage and influential editorials. Now it was mostly concerned with the question of what type of company would be suited for the task of constructing the rail line. Three types of companies were mentioned as possible choices: a state-owned company, a privately owned company, or a company of capital mixed "of the State with a company." Of the first, the editors suggested that generally, "in America, the governments, when they execute these same great works, do them at greater cost, very slowly, and in final result worse." A private company represents "the most simple system, most logical, equitable, equal for all countries, and the most productive of true wonders, of the marvels of our epoch. There has not been recently any important discovery that does not owe its application to private associations." The mixed company was looked on as unworkable. One can already see the strength of the Valparaíso business community and its capitalist mentality.

By 1846 Wheelwright's experience had undoubtedly equipped him with an ability to sense the potential realization of one of his projects as it came under the purview of public opinion. Knowing that the railroad measure would have difficulty passing congress, he gained the consent of a sufficient proportion of his future stockholders and, following many conferences with government officials, initiated a new plan.

A contract was signed by Wheelwright and Minister of Interior Manuel Camilo Vial in December 1846. It provided for a 30-year exclusive privilege. The government would give the necessary land free of charge except in the cities of Santiago and Valparaíso. Instead of a guaranteed 5 percent interest on capital invested, the contract provided for 5 percent on a maximum of 6 million pesos for 10 years from the start of operations, "and only for the sum that the road failed to produce . . . after deducting the costs of conservation and repair." After the 10-year period, all profits over 10 percent would go to repay the 5 percent guarantee until it was completely repaid. Rates were to be fixed by the company and the government jointly every 5 years, but for the first 5-year period, rates would be declared by the government. At the end of the 30-year monopoly the government could purchase the railroad according to certain explicit conditions stated in the contract.

Considering Chile's recent problems with North American copper interests during the 1950s and 1960s, it is probable that few Chileans would find their country's free-wielding strength in dealing with an earlier North American capitalist less than remarkable.

The contract was sent to the senate in June 1847, where it encountered severe criticism. President of the Senate Irarrázaval vigorously opposed the contract because of the 5 percent guarantee. But Minister of Interior Vial argued for the contract, even touching lightly and carefully on the positive nature of a foreign loan. In July the contract was approved "in general" and then subjected to the most minute inspection.

While the contract was in the senate, both the *Mercurio* and *Progreso* found a fertile field for their editorials. Early in July 1847 the *Progreso* took an official position critical of the plan's detractors. The paper suggested that the opposition's most solid point was its concern that the 5 percent guarantee would be an inexorable burden on the public treasury. Then, supposing the government would have to pay a part or all of the 5 percent, which seemed unlikely, the editors stated:

meanwhile industry and agriculture would take a prodigious turn, our products would be subject to more advantageous exchange rates, private fortunes would climb, property would increase in value; our fields would receive better cultivation and be planted with new, variated and valuable products; new industries would be born to nourish a new colony of Europeans that we would have in our bosom and from whom we would enjoy incalculable advantages.

This classically liberal, emphatically capitalist outlook was becoming manifestly characteristic of many influential Chileans by mid-nineteenth century and helps to account for the dominant position of foreigners in the nitrate industry by the end of the century.

The *Mercurio* also supported the contract and the 5 percent guarantee. The paper stated that the present annual value of the transportation trade between Valparaíso and Santiago was 1 million pesos. It seemed obvious to the editors that the company would earn more than 300,000 pesos; but if it did not, would not such a project be worth 200,000 or 100,000 pesos to the government? Although it might not produce a 5 percent profit in transportation, "it would produce 100 percent, 1,000 percent, in the development of agriculture, in the increment to commerce, in the advancement of industries, of the skills that it would introduce and spread; bringing the country 1,000 percent profit in areas distinct from transportation."

The chamber of deputies received the rail contract in July 1847 and subjected it at once to lengthy discussions. The session soon ran out. When it convened again in June 1848 its president, Manuel Montt, soon to be president of the republic, attacked the contract and postponed action on it until it was finally passed in 1849. It was soon signed into law.

In the ensuing months, Wheelwright found himself as yet unable to form a company. During the year 1850, his energetic efforts to form an Anglo-Chilean company were negated by economic dislocations in Europe and insurrection in Chile. He simply could not raise the capital. The Chilean government, which seemed on the verge of assuming an active role in the project by the end of 1849, no longer showed interest as it confronted more urgent political problems.

The situation altered markedly in 1851. All abstractions and details were relegated to a secondary position as the problem of how to raise the necessary capital became the single critical issue. At the end of May, President Bulnes authorized the formation of two commissions of outstanding citizens, one in Santiago and the other in Valparaíso, each charged with the task of finding ways to raise the necessary capital for the Santiago-Valparaíso railroad.

The newspapers were quick to regain the interest they, along with everyone else, had lost. And, as with the others, the main topic for discussion was the problem of raising the capital. The *Mercurio* contended that the road should be built with foreign capital. The paper was afraid that the retirement of 6 or 7 million pesos from local capital sources might produce a scarcity, force interest rates up, and cause less to be available for local needs. But it reported that public enthusiasm seemed overwhelmingly in favor of employing only local capital in constructing the line.

By 1851 there had been precedent for this. In 1849 Wheelwright had formed the Copiapó Railway Company for the construction of a line between Copiapó and the port of Caldera, a distance of about fifty miles. Both towns were in the desert province of Atacama, which achieved notoriety in 1832 when the famous Chañarcillo silver mines were discovered. At once the province became a favorite of migrating Chileans and foreigners. By mid-century there was a very affluent and powerful class of mining capitalists in the province. The miners wanted a railroad to connect the mining district with the port of Caldera.

Without any problems Wheelwright raised 750,000 pesos for the line. This was not an enormous amount of money when one considers that the Santiago-Valparaíso line required many times more. But it was a substantial amount; and it demonstrates that when local capitalists deemed it appropriate, they could go about the business of providing necessary improvements with little fanfare. There is an interesting sidelight to the list of original stock subscribers. Several of them were foreigners, like Edwards, Subercaseaux, and Wheelwright, but it appears that only one of them, Wheelwright, did not settle in Chile permanently. Descendants of most of the original subscribers were prominent figures in twenti-eth-century Chile.

With Wheelwright as the company's superintendent, work began on the line in early March 1850, and the line was opened to a test run in late December 1851. It was not, as Chileans generally claim, South America's first railroad, but it was a commendable achievement.

The Valparaíso commission made its report in July 1851, at a time when construction on the northern line was in full progress. It proposed that the government build the railroad entirely on its own behalf, using domestic rather than foreign loans as the basis for construction. The Santiago commission favored a *sociedad anónima,* formed in the country, with the government subscribing 2 million pesos worth of the proposed 4 million-peso issue, while never possessing more than one quarter of the votes. Now the *Mercurio* took a position favorable to the Valparaíso report, commenting, "The government is nothing else than the sovereignty of the nation, the agent created by the people to carry into effect works such as these, for which the people pay." Apparently, lead-ing forces of the Valparaíso business community had come to favor public construction of major internal improvements with domestic capital.

However, in August 1851 the basic proposals of the Santiago commission became law. A sociedad anónima would be formed with a basic capital of 4 million pesos, the government subscribing one-half the issue. Stocks were to replace a foreign loan and were to bear 8 percent interest.

The *Mercurio* was not optimistic. Faithful to its position that the government should build the line, it noted that merchants would be little inclined to buy stocks with a maximum interest of 8 percent, when on the open market they could expect at least 15 percent on their investments. Hacendados would not invest in the project because the present agricultural prosperity was not enough to balance the previous bad years, and with the present market excellent and a large demand from the United States, farmers needed all available capital for the production of cereals. "This means they *need* capital for their works." Likewise, the bankers could easily find more profitable areas for investment.

The *Mercurio* of Valparaíso has always been considered the organ of the port's merchant community. Here it had directly touched on one of the country's main economic problems. The scarcity of capital was not due principally to its appropriation by the world capitalist metropolises; it was due to the manner in which local capitalists invested their substantial capital and the manner in which the government taxed, that is, did not tax, its people. The organ of Chile's commercial community was calling for the government to build the railroad and build it entirely with domestic capital. The paper was advocating quite an advanced form of national capitalism.

It took until February 1852 for the government to announce the formation of a company to construct the rail line and to call for subscriptions. Wheelwright once again proposed a plan that would permit him to carry out the construction. The government was interested and immediately appointed a five-member commission to report on the new plan.

A company was formed in March to be capitalized at 7 million pesos, with the government subscribing 2 million pesos. Wheelwright was neither included in the conferences that led to the formation of the company nor given the contract to carry out the construction of the rail line. It would appear that he was maneuvered out of a contract by a small group of Chilean capitalists who were extraordinarily wealthy and self-assured. Three of the more important of them were Matías Cousiño, Angel Custodio Gallo, and Joshua Waddington. Supposedly, the three of them together subscribed 2 million pesos worth of stock. Cousiño and Gallo had made their fortunes in the northern mining industry, and Waddington, a naturalized Chilean, had made his in Valparaíso commerce.

The events and circumstances leading to the final formation of a company to build the Santiago-Valparaíso railroad do not suggest foreign imperialism or neocolonialism. The spirited boldness manifested by national capitalists and the domestic economic strength that supported their efforts are important factors for an understanding of what happened to the country's nitrate industry at the turn of the century.

The Santiago-Valparaíso railroad was not completed until 1863 and then only after the government took an even greater part in the financing, and Henry Meiggs arrived to direct the operation.

There was neocolonialism in Chile during the early national period in the sense that foreigners were active in the domestic economy, some making fortunes and returning home. Chilean production depended on foreign markets and foreign shipping and was subject to the vicissitudes of the world capitalist system. Domestic priorities, therefore, were sometimes determined abroad. There was neocolonialism also in the sense that Chilean development was sometimes heavily dependent on foreign capital and, therefore, on foreign influence. And it must have been terribly degrading for Chilean statesmen to be confronted by petitions from the foreign merchant community signed by the commander of the British naval forces in the Pacific. Yet it was not an extreme form of neocolonialism. Overall the Chileans did very well in their dealings with foreigners. This was, after all, the age of world capitalism and not world socialism. One might even say that the Chileans took good advantage of the foreigners and their capital. And we are left with the clear fact that a national consciousness and a national identity did develop. It even put Chile on the road to offensive war with other sovereign nations.

Chile's capitalism and its political liberalism served the country satisfactorily between 1810 and 1848. But then a new age dawned: it was the age of socialism and mass democracy. There were new ground rules, new criteria for what a society should be. Some Chileans realized this immediately; it took others a century.

6

NEW FORCES AND OLD CONCEPTS, 1848–1891

The introduction and popularization of new social concepts in Chile at mid-nineteenth century followed a prominent and vital artistic development, the famous literary movement of 1842. This movement started with the publication of two literary newspapers. The first, the *Revista de Valparaíso,* appeared in February. It was edited by an Argentine, Vicente Fidel López, in collaboration with two other Argentines, Juan María Gutiérrez and Juan Bautista Alberdi. It was unsuccessful in the sense that it endured only through six issues, but it managed to stir a significant literary debate. In April the *Museo de Ambas Américas* made its first appearance, also in Valparaíso and also directed by a foreigner, the Colombian Juan García del Río, a man of impressive credentials. This paper had a somewhat longer and more provocative life. At about the same time another foreigner, Domingo F. Sarmiento, joined the editorial staff of Valparaíso's *Mercurio* and expanded its literary content. By the end of the year 1842 Santiago had its first daily, the *Progreso,* edited by Sarmiento. Many of the foreigners, especially the Argentines, were political refugees who did not go out of their way to conceal their national identities as they became influential public personalities in Chile. But there was another group of foreigners, all distinguished scholars, including Bello, Domeyko, and Gay, some of whom had been in Chile more than a decade, who worked for the Chilean government and often with Chilean youth. These foreigners did not appear quite so obviously apart and threatening to the young Chileans as did the Argentines. Many of the Argentines were young and brash, whereas the older generation of foreigners were tutors to the new generation of Chilean intellectuals and not their competitors.

In February 1842 the young Chilean intellectuals formed the *Sociedad de Literatura*. In July the society began publishing its own literary paper, the *Semanario de Santiago*. A veritable literary battle was waged between the young Chileans and Argentines. The paper expired after six months and the society soon lost any effectiveness. However, by 1843 Chile was probably the leading literary center in South America.

One significant manifestation of the literary and intellectual movement of 1842 was the founding of the Liberal Party in 1849. The pelucón coalition lasted less than two decades. In fact it was attacked from within even before Prieto's first presidential term ended. By the late 1840s Chile had something approaching modern political parties. The old pelucones became the Conservatives and the reformists became the Liberals. The Liberals, inspired by the brilliant José Victorino Lastarria, urged suffrage reform and a more open press and opposed presidential authoritarianism.

Another important manifestation of the 1842 movement was the public appearance of the bright young intellectual and political agitator Francisco Bilbao. In 1843, when he was only twenty, he published *La esclavitud moderna,* a translation of Lamennais's work. The following year he published an article of his own, "Sociabilidad chilena," which brought him instant notoriety. It was an extremely emotional critique of Chile's colonial past, and it occasioned a public scandal. What caused him the most trouble probably was his attack on the established church. Bilbao was brought up on civil charges of blasphemy, immorality, and sedition. A trial was held in 1844, and the defendant was acquitted of the charge of sedition but was convicted of blasphemy and immorality and fined 1,200 pesos. Chile's youth had their first national hero: Bilbao was thrown out of law school. In the same year he left Chile for Europe, where he studied with leading French intellectuals. He returned to Chile in 1850, in time to become a prime mover in the revolt of 1851.[1]

[1] The revolt of 1851 had both social and federalist causes. Many supporters of the revolt, especially in Santiago, had distinct social revolutionary intentions, while the northern and southern provinces fought largely for

Chile's intellectual climate was greatly influenced at mid-nineteenth century by two young nationals with French backgrounds: Santiago Arcos and Bilbao. The former was the son of a Spanish soldier who had fought on the Spanish-American side of the independence movement and who had arrived in Chile with San Martín's Army of the Andes. Antonio Arcos had quite a successful financial career in Chile during the O'Higgins regime. After O'Higgins fell from power in 1823, Arcos moved to Rio de Janeiro and then to France, where he became a successful banker. After the July 1830 revolution in France, Arcos returned to Chile with his Chilean wife and four children. Santiago Arcos was born in 1822 and had lived in France only a few years, but perhaps this experience was enough to stimulate his lifelong interest in French matters. Even before the 1848 revolution and probably earlier than any other Chilean living within the country, he read the French Socialists and European utopianists. He is quite often referred to as Chile's first Communist. By 1850—before he was thirty years old—he was a leading and influential Chilean intellectual.

Francisco Bilbao studied with Michelet and Quinet and knew Lamennais. By 1850, when he was permitted to return to Chile, he was a social radical. He and Arcos were both dedicated to the destruction of Chile's social system, but neither appears to have been overly concerned with a specific plan for the future. In 1850, along with other, younger Chilean radicals, they formed the *Sociedad de la Igualdad,* an apolitical club devoted to the social reorganization of the country. Members had to recognize the sovereignty of reason, the sovereignty of the people in all political activity, and love and fraternity as the essence of morality. The Sociedad soon began publishing a newspaper, and before long the original members were joined by some older individuals experienced in previous revolts. Within months the Sociedad became

---

federalist reasons. Altogether this failed revolt, finally led by General José María de la Cruz, who had been recently defeated by Manuel Montt for the presidency, cost around 2,000 lives.

politically motivated and the focus of opposition to Manuel Montt, the government's presidential candidate. Before the end of the year the government closed the Sociedad and sent several opposition leaders into exile.

Chile did not get its social revolution at the middle of the nineteenth century, in fact, one could say it did not get one thereafter; and the efforts of Arcos and Bilbao really were to no avail. But the point is that by the middle of the nineteenth century the ideas and concepts of mass democracy already had been introduced into Chile. The twentieth century, however, has become the age of mass civilization, not elitism, the age of mass democracy, not individualistic liberalism. Liberalism and its economic counterpart, capitalism, no longer appear to be the combination of choice for the world's majority as are socialism and its political counterpart, mass democracy, even when this mass democracy is to be arrived at through the totalitarian dictatorship of the proletariat.

Chile did not feel the logical consequences of the challenge to liberal capitalism by the new mass democracy and its socialism for decades after the middle of the nineteenth century because it continued to enjoy the presence of one of liberal capitalism's most important foundation stones: economic abundance or the illusion of it. Chilean capitalism functioned on the basis of a myth. The myth was that the socially average person who applied himself with socially average industriousness could get his fair share of the quite visible abundance. By about 1890 the myth was being seen for what it really was, and an ever increasing portion of the population was becoming less and less impressed with the efficacy of capitalism.

During the four decades after the middle of the nineteenth century there were several signs that Chile was indeed blessed by an economic abundance. During the first two ten-year pelucón administrations (those of Prieto and Bulnes) the basis of a modern economic infrastructure was outlined, and during the third (that of Montt) it was consolidated and expanded. By 1861, after thirty years of pelucón leadership, the country had railroads, steamship lines, telegraphs, and banks.[2] There was a major colonization scheme for the south, although this was aimed mainly at foreigners. In some parts of the country there was a sizable and rapid increase in small landholders between 1860 and 1890. After the 1850s increased land values made it possible for many Chilean families to find smaller estates more economically advantageous than the traditionally larger ones. Many of the large estates were broken down into what have come to be called *fundos* thus making for a potentially more rational agriculture and at the same time making land available for others. The great age of Chilean agriculture during the nineteenth century ran from 1864 to 1875. It was a prosperous period, but it did not spawn the kind of rural oligarchy we have learned to associate with Spanish America during the century. Employing some guesswork, the *Mercurio* of Valparaíso in 1882 published the names of the fifty-nine largest personal fortunes in Chile. Its intent was to demonstrate the possible results available to a country of "order and freedom." Thirty-five of the largest fortunes belonged to miners, bankers, businessmen, and merchants. Only twenty-three of these over-a-million-peso-fortunes (at forty-eight pence) belonged to hacendados. Large landowning during the latter part of the nineteenth century in Chile was certainly not at all a stagnant affair. Many of the new and important landowners were primarily urban capitalists who drew their social standing, political power, and economic wealth centrally from their urban operations. Depressed agricultural prices starting in 1876 caused many estates to change hands and again made further land available to the new urban rich. Thus one segment of society, the politically active, had tangible reason to believe that capitalism was a perfectly appropriate and desirable

[2] During the short-lived wheat boom that followed upon the California gold rush a series of flour mills came into existence that were among the most technologically advanced in the world. That they failed to live up to expectations was due not to technology or expertise but to insurmountable local geographic obstacles in the face of increased world competition. See Arnold J. Bauer, "Chilean Rural Society in the Nineteenth Century" (unpublished doctoral dissertation, University of California, Berkeley, 1969), p. 29.

economic system for the country. And this applies to the many Chileans who made fortunes in the northern mining districts.

But there is another significant aspect to the mining and agricultural developments of the late nineteenth century. As a result of the War of the Pacific, 1879–1883, Chile not only acquired immensely valuable northern nitrate regions formerly belonging to Peru and Bolivia, but also a large mining proletariat. And in agriculture by 1890 there had occurred an impressive change to wage labor as a replacement of the traditional system of inquilinaje in parts of the country. While there was a genuine vertical and horizontal mobility for the upper classes with a promising flexibility, by 1890 a modern proletariat was coming into existence and even being organized, and this segment of society possessed increasingly greater numbers of people who were becoming increasingly less impressed with the appropriateness and desirability of capitalism. Few were yet doctrinaire radicals; most merely were searching out a better way of life. Until nearly the end of the nineteenth century there had been effective safety valve features in the Chilean economy such as the availability of cheap food and land and the possibility of emigration to prevent the establishment of a sizable landless and immobile proletariat that would have been subject to radicalization. But these options were closing with each decade as the population grew and urbanization increased. Chile started the century with fewer than a million people and finished it with more than 2½ million.

The period after 1848 was not only one of new social ideas in Chile, it was also the great age of classical economics, that is, of laissez faire capitalism. Between 1855 and 1863 the French liberal economist, Courcelle-Seneuil, in his capacity as advisor to the ministry of treasury, educated a whole generation of public and private leaders in the theory of laissez faire capitalism. Thus, just at a time that the state was finally taking a direct and active financial role in the construction of internal improvements, leading intellectuals such as Lastarria, Barros Arana, and Santa María were very much upset by the government's intent to sponsor financially major railroads. By the 1870s laissez faire capitalism was immensely popular in Chile. One must understand that this popularity was not artificial, that laissez faire capitalism was not forced on the Chileans but that it achieved its popularity because the Chilean economy encouraged such a theory. In the decade or so after the completion of the Santiago-Valparaíso railroad in 1863 Chilean agriculture witnessed an extravagant boom. In 1870 the Caracoles silver mining region was discovered and this gave the Chilean economy in general and the northern mining sector in particular a potent impetus. And although the country's position as a world leader in the production of copper was seriously undermined during the 1880s by discoveries in the United States, new nitrate deposits and territories more than offset this. Northern miners and government officials as well lived by trade. In 1854 about 66 percent of the government's revenue came from levies on foreign trade; in 1897, 97 percent of its revenues derived from this source.

This was an exceedingly confident period in Chilean history, and as will be shown, the soaring economy led the country into an imperialistic war. In the decades after 1850 Chile clearly had enough of the economic abundance or the illusion of it to support the concept of laissez faire capitalism. Vicente Pérez Rosales wrote, "I believed, as so many young men believe, who are poor but enamored, that merely taking a rural farm in rental, without any other resources than money borrowed at short term, with the spirit and desire of work, was enough to provide one's home with, in addition to his wife, happiness and wealth." This is the thinking, based on economic factors, that makes for a congenial acceptance of laissez faire capitalism. And it was this brand of capitalism which allowed the foreigners to participate freely in the country's mining industry. At first there appeared to be enough room for everyone, foreigners and Chileans alike, but by 1890 or so, with a government that understood that the general interests of the population required direct and massive government intervention in all aspects of public life, the foreign domination of the country's mining industry, the overwhelmingly primary source of the government's revenues, came to be seen by many in a much different light.

The nitrate industry was the backbone of the Chilean economy during the final decades of the nineteenth century, just as copper is today. But when nitrates first began to loom so large in the Chilean economy the primary deposits belonged to other countries. Chilean capitalists were quick to exploit the nitrate regions of Antofagasta and Tarapacá. José Santos Ossa and Francisco Puelma received a concession from Bolivia in 1866 for their *Compañia Explotadora del Desierto de Atacama,* established to exploit Bolivian nitrates and borax. The company soon became larger and more powerful with the addition of the important Chilean capitalist Augustín Edwards and the British-Peruvian-Chilean firm of Gibbs y Cía., already a significant financial force in the nitrate industry of Tarapacá. The new company became known as the *Compañia de Salitres y Ferrocarril de Antofagasta.* Additional nitrate deposits were being discovered and brought into operation all the time. In the early 1870s a Chilean explorer discovered the important deposit of El Toco. By 1872 Chilean capital was producing a little less nitrate than Peruvian capital and more than English and German capital, which already represented a considerable amount. Chilean capitalism had developed to such a degree that the country was now an exporter of capital to foreign countries. And much of this capital was actually generated and exported by Chilean nationals.

Before long the Bolivian and Peruvian nitrate industries became essentially a Chilean affair. Chilean capitalists and workers explored, established, and operated the nitrate districts of Antofagasta. They built the roads, railroads, and even the port of Antofagasta. Practically the entire desert population was Chilean. A census of 1878 showed that the municipality of Antofagasta contained 8,507 inhabitants, of which 6,554 were Chilean and 1,226 were Bolivian. The *Compañia de Salitres de Antofagasta* invested as much as 1 million pounds sterling in its foreign operations. Chileans invested a sizable amount of capital in the Peruvian region of Tarapacá, also. More than 10,000 Chilean workers were employed there.

The Chilean domination of the Peruvian and Bolivian nitrate industries led to tensions between the various national capitalists and their countries. Chilean explorers had also earlier discovered Bolivia's rich guano deposits. In 1866 Bolivia and Chile signed a boundary treaty in which the latter recognized the former's sovereignty over the guano territory and agreed to a northern boundary at 24 degrees latitude. Revenues produced from guano and other minerals found between 23 and 25 degrees would be shared equally between the two countries. Shortly after the treaty was signed Chilean explorers discovered the rich nitrate deposits near Antofagasta and then the silver mines of Caracoles. The Chileans requested permission from the Bolivian government to exploit these finds and were granted it. However, they were permitted to carry out their mining operations only under the financial arrangements stipulated in the 1866 treaty. Chilean capital and manpower literally invaded the region and soon Peru's Tarapacá mining district also. In 1873 Peru and Bolivia signed a secret offensive and defensive military treaty to protect against the actual loss of their mining territories to the Chilean flag. The following year Bolivia and Chile signed another treaty. In this one Chile gave up all rights north of 24 degrees in return for a promise that the Chilean capitalists in that region would not be confronted with new taxes. Just about this time the Peruvian government began nationalizing the nitrate industry in the province of Tarapacá, and Chileans lost mines, machinery, and income. In 1878 the Bolivian government, contrary to the provisions of the 1874 treaty, established new taxes on the Chilean producers of Antofagasta. The Chileans refused to pay and the Bolivian government determined to embargo their products and auction off their facilities. On the day in February 1879 when the auction was scheduled to take place, a small Chilean expeditionary force occupied the port of Antofagasta. Thus the famous War of the Pacific began between Chile on one side and Peru and Bolivia on the other. The allies outmanned Chile four to one at first in troops and two to one in population, but the Chileans won the war anyway. By the Treaty of Ancón, signed between Chile and Peru in 1883, Chile received ownership of the province of Tarapacá and permission to occupy Tacna and Arica. The following year a truce with Bolivia gave Chile sovereignty over the present province of Antofagasta.

Chile now had legal title to the mineral wealth which primed its economy during the last decades of the nineteenth century and which proved to be the mainstay of its economy during the twentieth century, copper now being the important product. It is at least a bit ironical that Chile's recent problems with copper and the question of nationalization would not exist in their present form were it not for this successful imperialistic war. In fact, it might have been Chileans who would have been threatened with nationalization.

In a surprisingly brief period the Chilean capitalists in the northern mining regions were replaced largely by foreigners. This was one of the most tragic moments in Chile's long economic history. At this point in their history Chileans had the capital, technology, and skilled workers to operate their mining industry as effectively as anyone else. Had the Chileans not lost their dominant position in their own mining establishment, it is more than likely they would not have fallen behind in capital, technology, and skilled workers and that many of their present social, political, and economic problems would be less severe.

Therefore, it ought to be made very clear why the Chileans lost out to the foreigners. Right from the start of the War of the Pacific, Chile controlled the important mining regions in question and resolved to use mining revenue to finance its military operations. In 1880 the government appointed a commission to study the problem of how mining operations should be carried out in the province of Tarapacá during the military occupation. But the commission, comprised of distinguished Chileans, made plans for the future also. The central question was whether the mining operations should be carried out under the present system of monopoly or under some other system. It should be borne in mind that the two most influential members of the commission, Marcial González and Zorobabel Rodríguez, were disciples of Courcelle-Seneuil and both were dedicated to the principles of laissez faire capitalism. The commission voted unanimously against the alternative of monopoly, noting that Chile should follow the first rule of good public economics, "which condemns all government intervention in the special domain of industry." There was also a significant financial factor which influenced the commission. The Peruvian government had made plans to pay for the nationalization of the Tarapacá mining industry with certificates backed by a foreign loan that as yet had not been subscribed. It was estimated that if the Chilean government were to operate the mining industry as a state monopoly, it would have to spend £5,419,264 to cancel the certificates issued by the Peruvian government in payment of its nationalization scheme. This enormous amount included also the mines of Tarapacá not yet nationalized and the mines of Antofagasta. A second commission soon favored ownership of the mines by private parties. In 1881 the government decreed that the mines of Tarapacá would be turned over to anyone able to produce Peruvian certificates with a face value of at least three-fourths the value of a given mine. As a consequence of the war and the financial community's belief that Chile would not honor the Peruvian debt, the nitrate certificates were selling at a fraction of their face value. After the government's decision was taken, an Englishman, John Thomas North, using capital supplied by Chilean sources, especially the Bank of Valparaíso, began buying up the Peruvian certificates and practically overnight became, as he liked to believe, the king of the nitrate industry. Francisco Encina has estimated that in 1878 the capital of Americanized Englishmen invested in the nitrate industry amounted to 13 percent of the total, while Peruvian-Chilean capital represented 67 percent, with 20 percent belonging to foreigners economically nationalized. By August 1884 Peruvian capital had been eliminated, Chilean capital reduced to 36 percent of the total, English capital increased to 34 percent, and the capital of Europeans not nationalized brought to 30 percent. By the end of 1901 English capital represented 55 percent of the total, nonnationalized European capital amounted to 30 percent, and Chileans themselves had only 15 percent of the total investment.[3]

[3] However, the British consul in Iquique estimated that in 1910 British capital invested in the Chilean nitrate industry amounted to £10,700,000, Chilean capital, £10,500,000, German capital, £3,300,000, and the capital of other national groups, £3,000,000. If these figures are correct then Chileans were not entirely out of the picture, but the amount of

This conspicuous change came about for several reasons. Many Chileans, especially prominent ones, were keenly influenced by the ideas of laissez faire capitalism and opposed the creation of a state nitrate monopoly. The costs of fighting the War of the Pacific in addition to the monumental debt the government would have had to assume—according to its own principles—in covering the Peruvian nitrate certificates surely must have frightened many a government official and member of the two commissions. And finally, one must remember that most Chileans were not afraid of having foreigners participate in their economic development. Traditionally foreigners had been handled very well by Chilean governments. And in this case the territories involved were actually foreign territories in which the Chileans themselves had been functioning as foreigners. It must be made clear that the foreign domination of the Chilean nitrate industry was not brought about by a group of imperialists, and it was not the result of a direct effort at colonialism. It occurred because the Chileans were practicing a brand of capitalism that permitted it. It was a capitalism suited to the era in which it was conceived and it functioned more or less well during the course of the nineteenth century. But it was not equipped to meet the social demands made on it during the twentieth century. In fact, the nitrate affair might well be taken as the final flourish of an economic rationale that had brought Chile an enviable prosperity and stability but which was not suited to the social concepts of the new century.

The limitations of Chile's nineteenth-century capitalism became obvious or, at least, should have become obvious during the presidency of José Manuel Balmaceda, which began in 1886 and terminated with his suicide in 1891. Balmaceda became president at a time of great economic prosperity for Chile. Before the War of the Pacific, annual state revenues amounted to about 15 million pesos, but in 1887 these had reached about 45 million pesos. Balmaceda was a state interventionist, one who believed that only

---

foreign investment and control would still impress Chileans as having been too great.

the state could carry out the economic and social reforms necessary for development. He wanted to provide internal improvements, to stimulate and protect local industry, to improve educational facilities, to increase wages, to reform the tax system. In short, he wanted to bring Chile full steam into the twentieth century. Though impressive, state revenues were not sufficient to support such a dynamic and progressive program. To pay for all this he proposed the nationalization of the Tarapacá nitrate industry and, additionally, the Tarapacá railway system. Both were largely owned and controlled by foreigners.

One result of Balmaceda's ambitious program and his thoughts on paying for it was the revolt of 1891, which ended in his death and the institution of the parliamentary republic. Quite often writers, especially those of the left, mention the revolt of 1891 essentially to stress the pernicious role foreigners like North played in opposing Balmaceda and his progressive plans for the economic and social development of Chile, plans that would have eliminated them from the Chilean scene.[4] The foreigners are often pictured as the villains in this calamitous rebellion, one that left over 10,000 Chileans dead. There is little doubt that foreigners with their nitrate profits made financial contributions to the congressional cause and helped the revolt succeed. The revolt was an unusually complicated one, however, and it is unfairly simplistic to focus on the foreigners to the exclusion of the other significant factors in the rebellion.

The emphasis on the foreigners and Balmaceda's social and economic program is a relatively recent one. Traditionally, historians have stressed the constitutional nature of the conflict between Balmaceda and the congress. The new emphasis is certainly a valid corrective to the older one, but both leave much to be desired. Even before Balmaceda became president the congress was in the process of asserting itself, of making itself a more

---

[4] For the historiography of the Balmaceda revolt see Harold Blakemore, "The Chilean Revolution of 1891 and Its Historiography," *Hispanic American Historical Review* vol. 45, no. 3 (August 1965).

meaningful institution of government and a more equal partner to the president.

Though the constitution of 1833 invested the congress with considerable power, the first pelucón presidents managed to govern as authoritarians. It was, in fact, presidential authoritarianism that caused a split in the pelucón coalition and the generation of several contending political parties. By the end of the Bulnes administration there were Conservatives and Liberals. By the end of the Montt administration there were Conservatives, Liberals, and Nationals. But now there was also a strong anticlerical movement in Chile, one that caused a further split in the old alliance. The hard-lining pelucones stayed in the Conservative party, which had elected Montt. Those who desired church reform and wanted to curtail presidential powers joined the Liberal party. But in 1857 moderate Liberals and Conservatives formed the National party which, for the moment, became the party of the government. José Joaquín Pérez was elected president in 1861 as the candidate of the National party, but he soon turned for support to a Liberal-Conservative fusion. Early in the Pérez administration the Radical party was created. It would develop into one of the country's most significant and powerful parties and would play a pivotal role in Chilean politics to the present day. Initially it was the party of the northern mining capitalists and northern and southern federalists. Later it became the party of the middle class. In the 1860s and 1870s it was the most progressive of the leading parties, opposing presidential authoritarianism, desiring constitutional reforms, notably suffrage clauses, and fighting for church reforms. If it was a "radical" party, yet it was not a democratic party. Its liberalism was nineteenth-century liberalism.

During the 1860s the central issue separating the major parties was theological. The more progressive parties favored separation of church and state, abolition of the church fuero, secularization of cemeteries, and lay marriages. The progressive forces managed only limited successes.[5]

[5] The fuero was ended and Catholic cemeteries were opened to non-Catholics. The progressives had wanted the establishment of non-Catholic cemeteries.

Political issues also separated the parties, with the Radicals again being the most progressive. The requirements for the franchise were reduced. Presidential powers were curtailed and the term limited to one five-year period at a time rather than two consecutive five-year periods. Federico Errázuriz Zañartu served the first five-year term, 1871–1875. During his administration the Liberal-Conservative fusion broke apart and a Liberal Alliance of all three parties was formed. The Democratic party was formed in 1887. It attracted support from some members of the growing middle class, from artisans, and even from some urban proletarians. Though it was the most radical of all the major parties, it did not effectively become the party of the people.

Clearly there was a conflict building between the president and the congress before Balmaceda announced his ambitious program. In 1890 the conflict centered around the congressional desire to influence the president's selection of his ministers. To back itself up the congress refused to authorize the president to collect taxes. Balmaceda gave in and appointed a cabinet satisfactory to the congress. The congress had thus effected a giant step toward establishing ministerial responsibility. But with congress soon out of session the president dismissed this cabinet and replaced it with one of his own. Since it was not in session the congress could not do anything official about this. However, the appropriation bill for 1891 had not yet been approved and to secure authorization the president would have had to convene congress. Consequently, he merely declared that the appropriation bill for the previous year would be in effect for 1891 also. The congress responded a few days later by revolting. With the support of the navy the congressional revolutionaries established a government in Iquique. They soon controlled all the mining provinces of the north, where they were supported by the miners and their workers. It took the congressional forces about eight months to win the war.

There can be no doubt that the revolt of 1891 was in part, at least, caused by the very real constitutional crisis produced by the conflict between congress and the president. Yet it is also certain that congressional opposition to the president was inspired in some cases by Balmaceda's progressive plans. Foreigners or no, the revolt would likely have occurred. The president's plans for nationalization of the northern nitrate industry would have affected Chilean capitalists just as much as it did the foreigners. In fact, the foreign issue seems quite incidental to the revolt. That the nitrate mine workers supported the revolt does not mean they did so strictly because they themselves were controlled by the foreign mine owners. During the great strike of 1890, finally put down by Balmaceda's government troops, thousands of northern workers were killed. Perhaps this induced the workers to oppose the executive forces or at least made the mine owners appear as the lesser of two evils.

There is also the issue of paper money. For some time before the revolt the government had been printing paper money to cover its expenses. It is generally assumed that this policy was favored by the landed rich, those who could sell their products for hard currency, buy depreciated paper, and then pay off debts. Many members of the landed rich did, in fact, fight against Balmaceda, but paper money probably was not the central issue for them since post-Balmaceda governments made strenuous efforts to get back on a metallic standard and raise the value of the peso in reference to the pound sterling.

What is probably more important for the revolt of 1891 is that Balmaceda had also proposed the establishment of a national bank, something that implied the nationalization of credit. This would have seriously undermined the financial position of the country's leading private bankers, people who ended up supporting the congressional forces. This question of banking was not related directly to foreigners or the foreign mining interests. It was strictly a Chilean national issue.

Thus there was no single cause of the revolt, no one factor that might be charged with responsibility for the disruption. The revolt was a watershed in Chilean history. The old capitalism could no longer satisfy the needs of the Chilean society. That foreigners were involved in the old capitalism's last great effort to sustain itself is beside the point. In effect Chilean society was pointedly different in 1890 from what it had been even only a few decades earlier. A party with Marxist overtones had been formed prior to the revolt. A major and bloody strike had occurred. Balmaceda's program was attuned to the requirements of Chilean society at large, but one can only conjecture about the country's eventual fate had it been adopted.

PART III
THE TWENTIETH CENTURY

7
THE ROAD TO SOCIALISM

The congressional revolt of 1891 was a civil war rather than a revolution. Though Balmaceda's wishful programs would have had social impact, he was not the champion of the lower classes, nor were the basic issues of the war linked directly to social reform. Apart from the fact that Balmaceda's plans were cast aside, the fundamental alteration in Chilean life was political. The old pelucón system of balanced powers had appeared to many Chileans as being tilted in favor of the president; now the victorious congressional forces thoroughly vitiated presidential authority and instituted the famous parliamentary republic that endured until 1920 or, more precisely, until the promulgation of the constitution of 1925.

The early twentieth century was a time of strong congresses, weak presidents, and government by coalition. Already by 1891 there were five major political parties, Conservative, Liberal, National, Radical, and Democratic. Two more were added soon thereafter. However, few serious issues separated the parties. The Conservatives and Radicals were at odds over both religion and education. The former favored an established church and an educational system free of government interference. The latter favored separation of church and state and an educational structure entirely supervised by the government, one that would require attendance to a certain age and be free and secular.

Though the leading parties were not significantly different in their aspirations, the period of the parliamentary republic was, nevertheless, marked by important social and political change. At one level there was the obvious fact that the congress was running the government and that even such a strong-minded president as Pedro Montt (1906–1910) could not successfully steer his programs through a maze of congressional factions. Presidential efforts were further encumbered by congressional censure of ministers and frequent changes in cabinets. In the 55 years following 1831 there were 31 cabinets, but in the 33 years following the establishment of the parliamentary republic there were over 120 cabinets with a total of more than 500 ministers. But there was a more subtle change taking place in the Chilean political system. The active citizenry was expanding and the scrupulous preservation of freedom of expression during the parliamentary period allowed it to receive a varied and often provocative political education.

As the election of 1920 demonstrated, many Chileans were becoming dissatisfied with parliamentary rule and the blatant electoral corruption that characterized it. Both the growing middle class (though it still lacked the homogeneity and class consciousness necessary for concerted political action) and the enlarged proletariat were developing a political awareness that would help bring on a new age in Chilean politics only three decades after the establishment of the parliamentary republic.

The parliamentary period was one of fundamental social change. The Chilean population was growing rapidly. By 1907 there were 3,250,000 people, 43 percent of whom lived in urban centers of at least 1,000 people. This population growth, along with an intense urbanization, contributed to the expansion of both the middle class and the proletariat. Though the old patriarchal system of electoral influence continued to preside in rural regions, and there was electoral corruption throughout the country, the growing urban middle class and the urban and mining proletariat were able to play a significant role in electing a reformist president in 1920.

The nature of the social change taking place during the parliamentary period is typified by the labor movement. We have already spoken of the important mining strike of 1890. The first important strike of the twentieth century was carried out by the maritime workers of Valparaíso in 1903. This strike also had to be put down by government troops. In 1905 the working classes of Santiago protested the rising cost of living, especially the high cost of meat. After unsuccessfully petitioning the government, the workers attacked some speculators and shops. Finally, they attacked police headquarters and actually controlled Santiago for two days. But the government got its forces together and regained control. Probably as many as 200 workers lost their lives. There was a major strike in Antofagasta in 1906, and the famous Iquique nitrate miners' strike occurred the following year. In the Iquique strike some 2,000 people were killed. In 1909 alone there were 29 important strikes throughout the country. Between 1911 and 1920 there were nearly 300 strikes in which more than 150,000 workers took part. Times had indeed changed, almost overnight.

Though labor was being organized, the political activities of the Chilean working classes were yet to be coordinated. Since the middle of the nineteenth century there had existed mutual benefit societies of workers that looked after some of the personal needs of the members without getting into the issues later taken up by full-fledged labor unions. In 1906 there were more than 200 of these societies. In the early twentieth century a new and more aggressive society, the *Mancomunal,* made its appearance. Working-class newspapers throughout the country aided the movement.

Several Chileans, most notably Luis Emilio Recabarren, were dedicated to organizing the workers into modern unions and political parties. The Chilean Workers Federation—though not at first very radical—was founded in 1909.[1] In 1912 Recabarren founded the country's first modern working-class political party, the Socialist Workers party. In 1921 he took the Chilean Workers Federation into Moscow's international trade union movement. The following year the Socialist Workers Party became the Communist party of Chile and joined the Third International. Chile's working-class parties are probably the only ones in Latin America to have grown directly out of the working-class movement. It is perhaps fitting that they were the first to elect a Marxist president in a truly free election. Because the traditional political parties did

[1] Since the 1950s the most important workers federation has been the *Central Unica de Trabajadores de Chile* (CUTCH).

not take up the cause of the workers, the workers themselves were forced to create and maintain their own parties. This failure on the part of the older parties, including the Democratic party, to meet the needs of millions of Chileans is still reverberating.

With the congressional elections of 1918 the parliamentary republic began to crumble. Chileans now sent reform-minded Liberal Alliance candidates (comprising Radicals, Liberals, Democrats, and Balmacedists) to congress and presaged the election of Arturo Alessandri—the "Lion of Tarapacá"—to the presidency in 1920.

The election of Alessandri as president in 1920 announced the emergence of modern Chile. Alessandri promised nothing less than a forceful revision of the Chilean constitutional and capitalist systems. Though in the final analysis he may not have lived up to his advance billing, Chile was never the same again. Alessandri was born in 1868 and won a law degree in 1893 with a thesis that explored the issue of low-cost working-class housing. As a corporate lawyer he manifested a modest interest in social reform. In 1897 he was elected a congressional deputy from Curicó, to the south of Santiago, and the following year he served briefly as a cabinet minister, as he did again in 1913. But it was not until he ran for the senate from the northern mining district of Tarapacá in 1915 that he became the vigorous and avowed advocate of social justice. With the Liberal Alliance congressional victory of 1918 Alessandri served briefly as minister of interior.

Supported by the Liberal Alliance, Alessandri won a tightly contested presidential battle in 1920 and brought hope of a new era of reform. His campaign was aimed especially at the growing lower and middle classes, but there were people from all social strata who found something exciting in Alessandri's bold challenge to the old system, in his promise of social and constitutional reform. In fact, with only about 8 percent of the population voting in that era and with literally thousands of workers who were agitated by the presidential campaign not voting, Alessandri's victory cannot be attributed entirely to the support of the proletariat or even the middle class.

Economic conditions in Chile after the termination of World War I certainly suggested the need of imaginative and vigorous reform. The armistice signed in 1918 brought an end to the momentarily revived nitrate industry. As nitrate mines closed, thousands of miners were thrown out of their jobs, as were workers in related industries and services, such as maritime workers. As a reaction to this situation strikes were commonplace. In 1919 a state of siege had to be declared to control labor unrest in mining areas. Just three months before the election of 1920 coal miners in the province of Concepción went on strike, and without coal the nation's railroads closed down. The strike lasted over eighty days. Workers struck in Valparaíso and in southern Magallanes and elsewhere.

In this turbulent milieu Alessandri promised constitutional reforms to end congressional dominance of the central government. To ameliorate the depressing social conditions of the Chilean workers he promised the institution of social security, a progressive labor code, low-cost housing, a modern educational system, and women's rights. He insisted on state control of banks and insurance companies and proposed to stabilize the monetary system.

For a variety of reasons Alessandri was unable at first to deliver on his promises. Though the Liberal Alliance controlled the chamber of deputies, it did not control the senate, and the senate proved recalcitrant in the face of such sweeping reform. The Liberal Alliance itself was fractured and by March 1921 had momentarily lost effectiveness. The president was left for the time being without the support of a commanding coalition. But perhaps most importantly, upon taking office Alessandri was confronted by the postwar depression that threatened stability and postponed reform in many countries.

It was indeed a direful depression that greeted the new president. There was widespread unemployment among mine, factory, and maritime workers. In Santiago by the end of 1921 more than 40,000 unemployed workers (an unusually high number) had applied for public assistance during the year. Paralyzing general strikes gripped Santiago and Valparaíso in June and dozens of other more selected actions throughout the year played havoc with ordinary business and personal activities all over the country. There were not only crippling strikes, but also equally disturbing lockouts. In November a mass gathering of workers in Santiago celebrated the fourth anniversary of the Bolshevik Revolution and was treated to an array of inflammatory leftist rhetoric. At least one senator encouraged the workers to overthrow the government. For those who were fortunate enough to hold jobs, the rising inflation often frustrated optimism. With wages remaining relatively stable, the value of the peso dropped from 27 cents (U.S.) in 1919 to 9 cents in 1924. To complicate the situation nitrate sales fell precipitously at the same time that the world price plummeted. (Alessandri told congress in January 1922 that more than 47,000 workers lost their jobs in the nitrate industry, more than 9,000 in copper, and some 1,200 in coal.)

It was in this atmosphere that Alessandri proposed his political and social changes. Addressing congress on June 1, 1921, he urged the transformation of the senate into a consultative body, the right of the president to dissolve the chamber, and the direct election of the president. In his attempt to restore the powers of the presidency he insisted that congress be deprived of its ability to censure members of the cabinet, one of the foundation stones of the parliamentary republic. He also urged the separation of church and state.

Though Alessandri may have been somewhat more concerned with terminating the parliamentary system than with social reform at this moment, his interest in the latter field was still pronounced. In the same congressional message he urged a broad policy of advanced social legislation, including restrictions on the working day and on child and female labor. His proposals included recognition of unions and their right to strike and accident, health, and old-age insurance. (But his proposals also included restrictions on wages.) The president wanted new property and income taxes, a tighter control over banks and insurance companies, and development of the merchant marine.

Clearly, Alessandri was a progressive national capitalist rather than a Socialist. He was proposing to enhance the capitalist system by attuning it to the needs of a greater number of Chileans than it had been before. He was not proposing to overthrow it.

Even so the president had the most limited success in implementing both his constitutional and socioeconomic reforms. Tax reforms and protective legislation for both industry and labor were enacted, but this only scratched the surface of his program.

Underscoring the absence of meaningful and effective socioeconomic reform was the president's helplessness at the hands of a strong and aggressive congress. During his first four years in office Alessandri had to reorganize his cabinet more than a dozen times, often as the result of congressional censure. And all the while the economic crisis continued generally unabated. Widespread unemployment, including governmental layoffs, and finally wage reductions were beginning to appear endemic.

It took until early 1924 for the Liberal Alliance to gain majorities in both houses of congress. In return for the passage of some significant legislation Alessandri made an informal agreement with the Conservatives not to intervene in the congressional elections of 1924. But as the election approached and the seating of a favorable congress appeared a clear possibility, the agreement proved to be more than Alessandri could abide. The Lion of Tarapacá had roar left in him even after four desultory years in office. Not only did he personally campaign, urging the election of reform-minded candidates, he used army and police forces to disrupt the opposition's political meetings and keep their voters from the polls.

The congressional election of 1924 potentially could have been one of the most consequential in Chilean history. Not only did a revived Liberal Alliance capture a majority in both houses, it sent to congress an impressive number of people genuinely concerned with socioeconomic reform. However, they were not quite so dedicated to Alessandri's constitutional ideas. According to the constitution, congressmen were to receive no salaries. This was not an unreasonable arrangement during the nineteenth century, when it was taken for granted that anyone elected to congress would be able to support himself while serving the country. Now with people from all walks of life being elected to congress, a change was needed. On this issue, which was indeed constitutional, both congress and the president agreed. But, rather than alter the constitution directly, in September the congress passed legislation providing for reimbursement of expenses incurred by the congressmen. This was tantamount to the enactment of salaries, and it was a reform that distressed many sections of society, especially the military.

The congress chose to pass its salary reform before confronting the more urgent aspects of Alessandri's program, and at a time when the country's dismal economic performance appeared unable to afford it. By September the congress had been in session long enough to have enacted the president's entire program, but internal dissension and procedural haggling within the legislature precluded the possibility of serious reform. Not only was congress's first reform an entirely selfish one, it was passed without commensurate regard for the economic plight of the military. This affront to a widespread desire for reform coupled with a seemingly callous disregard for the woefully inadequate military salaries prompted the military to intervene directly in the political life of the country for the first time in nearly a century. In the revolts of 1851 and 1891 military forces fought on one side or another, but now the army was acting on its own behalf.

During the twentieth century the social composition of the Chilean military altered radically. By 1924 it had lost its earlier patrician overtones. Officers, especially in the army, were now largely of middle-class origin, and their men were of proletarian origin. Willing to intervene in politics, together they formed a powerful force for reform.

Even before September 1924 there was indication that the military was losing its traditional political neutrality. As early as 1907 the secret *Liga Militar* was formed by army officers and within a few years counted members from all parts of the country. The *Liga* was concerned about the country's ineffectual political organization, to the point of considering a *coup*. In 1912 a similar *Liga Naval,* proposing a broad policy of socioeconomic reform, actually planned a *coup* against the government but did not carry it out. There was also a significant military conspiracy in 1919. Its leaders were tried and punished by the government.

In 1924 a secret military-civilian society called TEA (Tenacity, Enthusiasm, Abnegation) conspired to overthrow the government. The society was formed of prominent national figures. Its planned *coup* never materialized. While the TEA was forming, groups of middle- and junior-grade officers from the Santiago garrison began meeting to discuss their own cheerless situation. These younger army officers were especially concerned about the inept congress and its determination to circumvent the constitution in order to provide salaries for its members at a time when government and military personnel had not been paid for months. The officers, very aware of recent political interventions by the military in Spain and Brazil, entered politics in early September.

On September 2 a group of some fifty of these junior officers took seats in the senate gallery to hear the final debates of the congressional salary reform. With great enthusiasm they let their disapproval be known. On the following day another group of army officers entered the senate gallery to follow the debates. Many members of the senate and government considered these acts provocative and called for discipline. In the evening of September 5 the army officers made demands on the president. Among other things they wanted the salary reform bill which had passed through congress vetoed. On the same day a military junta was formed to direct the army's political activities. On September 8 congress met to vote on requests made by the army. The evening before Alessandri, responding to the military demands, vetoed the congressional salary reform bill. Now the congress, in remarkably short time, passed all the legislation proposed by the army, which amounted to Alessandri's socioeconomic program. Not only did the legislation protect labor and unions, improve working conditions, and provide working-class health insurance, it enlarged the army and raised military salaries.

With its program passed the military junta might well have dissolved and permitted its supporters to remove themselves from politics. The junta chose, however, to continue its guidance over the civilian government. Alessandri, in turn, refused to share his authority with the military, and he resigned on September 8. The junta attempted to get him to take a leave of absence, but the president would settle for nothing less than full resignation. Late in the same day that congress passed the promising reform program, Alessandri requested asylum in the United States embassy. Two days later he left the country. A newly formed military junta was now left in control of the government, and on September 11 it closed the congress. The calm, bloodless overthrow of civilian government won surprisingly wide support throughout the country and occasioned relatively little protest. In fact, Communist party leader Luis Emilio Recabarren had generous praise for the new military government, believing it to be an important step forward for Chilean workers.

On January 22, 1925, a second military *coup* brought a new and more radical junta into power. Major Carlos Ibáñez del Campo, forty-six years old and facing a less than brilliant future in the army, now became the preeminent force in the military reform movement. The new junta, along with other influential groups, urged Alessandri, then resident in Rome, to return to Chile and head the government. Alessandri was pleased but made it clear that he would return only if a civilian government was established and the military would resume its traditional role in the Chilean political system. He also wanted the convocation of a convention to write a new constitution and prepare for the election of a new president.

On January 27 a new provisional junta was created to govern the country until Alessandri's return from Europe. The junta was headed by a civilian, Emilio Bello Codesido, Balmaceda's son-in-law, who was given the title of vice president. Between January 28 and March 20, 1925, the Bello government decreed more than 200 laws, many of which were strikingly progressive. A graduated income tax was established, advanced labor legislation promulgated, and plans laid for the construction of low-cost housing.

Alessandri returned to Chile on March 20 and immediately took control of the government. The president's central concern now was constitutional reform and shortly the constitution of 1925, still in force today, was promulgated. While maintaining the traditional Chilean civil liberties, the new organic code destroyed the parliamentary system and restored the balance of powers between congress and president. The congress, still composed of a senate and a chamber of deputies, no longer could remove ministers through censure. (An impeachment process was provided for, however.) The presidential term was lengthened to six years with no immediate reelection, and the president was now to be elected by direct vote. (There is no vice president in the Chilean system. The minister of interior is next in line to succeed the president.) One of the bases of the parliamentary republic was congressional control over state finances, thus allowing the congress considerable leverage in dealing with the chief executive. The new code ended this predicament for the president by giving him effective control over finances. He no longer needed periodic authorization for the collection of taxes and payment of the military. Nor would he be left without a budget, as Balmaceda was. If congress did not approve or alter the president's national budget within four months of presentation, it would go into effect automatically.

The constitution provided other notable reforms. Church and state were finally separated and freedom of conscience guaranteed. The nineteenth-century liberal concept of private property rights was overturned: private property rights were subject to a broader social interpretation; they could be limited when social progress made it necessary. In principle the constitution advocated not only social progress but at least a minimum standard of living for all Chileans.

With the constitution of 1925 accepted, the parliamentary republic was over. There had been social and political change during the course of its three and a half decades. There also occurred a subtle but fundamental economic change. Foreigners slowly and unobtrusively purchased control of a sector of the economy that was not very promising at the time but which became the mainstay of the economy later. This was the copper industry.

During the late nineteenth and early twentieth centuries nitrate was king, and the revenues it brought the Chilean government financed many of its activities and supported its bureaucracy. Copper had been a major factor in the Chilean economy, and as late as 1880 the country had been a leading exporter of the mineral. After 1880 more efficient producers in other countries who could market copper with lower costs began to supersede the Chileans. Prices rose briefly around the turn of the century on the world market, and this helped the Chileans, but the prices became depressed once again. Chilean mines were failing in large numbers. However, during the first decade of the twentieth century a virtual revolution in copper technology made it worthwhile to work low-grade ore (common in Chile) on the basis of advanced, capital-intensive technology and a vertical operation including extraction, concentration, and smelting. The Chilean copper mines began to attract foreign attention, although even as late as 1913 copper was a minor factor in the Chilean economy when compared with nitrates.

Chilean copper production entered its modern age with the entrance of the Braden Copper Company into the lagging industry in 1904. Braden purchased a mountain of ore to the southeast of Santiago which today is the El Teniente mine, the first component of Chile's *Gran Minería*. More capital was required than even Braden could manage, and in 1908 he sold control of his company to the Guggenheims, who in 1915 transferred control of El Teniente to their own Kennecott Copper Corporation (making Braden a subsidiary of Kennecott). In 1911 the Guggenheim interests purchased control of a property that became the famous Chuquicamata mine, to the northeast of the port of Antofagasta. Chuquicamata became the second component of the Gran Minería and the largest open-pit mine in the world. In 1923 the Guggenheims sold Chuquicamata to the Anaconda Copper Mining Company to raise capital for their own nitrate ventures. (In 1913 Bethlehem Steel received a thirty-year concession to work Chile's iron ore deposits, giving it monopolistic control over Chilean iron ore production until the mid-1950s.) In 1916 the Andes Copper Mining Company, a subsidiary of Anaconda, was formed to work mines in the region of Potrerillos, to the southeast of Chuquicamata. This was the third and final component of the Gran Minería.

Thus, during the parliamentary republic Chile's largest copper mining operations had come under foreign control. By the end of the First World War the nitrate boom was over, and although nitrates continued to play a significant role in the economy for some time to come, copper was about to become king. When copper did become a prominent industry once again, it was largely dominated by foreigners.

With the promulgation of the constitution of 1925 Chile did not enter a period of presidential stability. Having achieved his constitutional reforms, Alessandri resigned even before the end of the year. Emiliano Figueroa was elected president, but he served only until his own resignation in May 1927. Figueroa was not reformist enough for many of his colleagues, especially Minister of War and then Minister of Interior Colonel Ibáñez. Shortly after Figueroa resigned, Ibáñez was elected president by a landslide majority in a notably free and honest election. Only about a quarter of a million votes were cast, but Ibáñez received 98 percent of them.

Ibáñez's first administration was one of the most controversial in Chilean history. Politically it was a forceful dictatorship. The president governed generally as he wished, throwing aside civil liberties and frustrating representative government. (Although his training was military, his government was not a military government.) It was an authoritarianism of action rather than words, of progress rather than retardation. Ibáñez guided one of the most impressive internal improvements schemes in modern Latin American history. Highways were built, sewer systems constructed, ports modernized, and public utilities improved. There was a massive reconstruction of the Chilean infrastructure. The president tried to increase agricultural productivity by encouraging European immigration, improving credit facilities, and involving the administration slightly in land reform. Similar initiative was shown in the critical field of public education. Elementary schools were opened throughout the country, with 5 times more being spent on public education than had been spent in 1920. By 1931 some 56 percent of the population was literate. Twice as many students could now find room in a school as could a decade earlier.

Ibáñez opened not only elementary schools, but normal, technical, and commercial schools as well. One of the administration's most progressive educational reforms made the University of Chile autonomous.

Ibáñez seemed to be doing something for everyone (including the military, who quite expectedly shared in the largesse); everyone, that is, except the political opposition on both sides of him. Political leaders were exiled or imprisoned and public expression of opinion severely curtailed.

To pay for his attractive programs Ibáñez relied on monumental foreign loans and the stimulating flow of foreign capital into the mining industry. At the time of the Wall Street crash in 1929 the Chilean economy was impressively strong, but almost overnight the market for the country's nitrates and copper dried up. No economy in the world suffered more from the depression than the Chilean. To stem the tide the government created COSACH, the *Compañía de Salitre de Chile,* in June 1930 to supervise nitrate production and organize its sale on the world market. COSACH was formed on the basis of government and private capital, both Chilean and foreign. Not only did it fail to stabilize the price of Chilean nitrate, it allowed the further penetration of United States private capital into the Chilean nitrate industry. By 1930 the Guggenheim interests already controlled about 70 percent of the country's nitrate production.

With the price of nitrate falling and the international bankers no longer able to continue the nourishing supply of development dollars flowing into Chile, Ibáñez was in serious trouble. The internal improvements program was curtailed and social services reduced. Taxes were raised, tens of thousands of workers thrown out of their jobs, and wages were reduced once again for many of the fortunate ones who kept their jobs.

On July 22, 1931, a general strike was planned by professional and white-collar workers determined to force Ibáñez's resignation. On the same day the cabinet voted to close all banks. And that day a group of students took control of the main building of the University of Chile and started shooting at the police outside. On the next day the physicians of Santiago struck. On July 24 lawyers joined the Santiago strike. Two days later Ibáñez resigned and went into exile.

For several years Ibáñez had managed to satisfy practically the entire citizenry. The internal improvements program was a source of pride and jobs, and it was a stimulus to the economy. Ibáñez enforced social legislation that had lain moribund on the books for years, legislation that now took on meaning. Those on both extreme sides of him politically doubtless found little comfort in his programs and reforms; they suffered his constant persecution. In the last analysis Ibáñez's progress was superficial and based on artificial strengths. It did not manage to alter the fundamental socioeconomic structure that had caused such discontent and that continued to do so for decades after Ibáñez fell from power. The military, whose authoritarian and pragmatic ways could be enviably efficient, had now had their chance to make essential change. They too failed.

For fifteen months after the fall of the Ibáñez dictatorship the country was plagued by intense political and social perturbation. Governments came and went with unreasonable rapidity; there were general strikes and further military machinations, including a naval revolt. With the resignation of Ibáñez a new presidential election was held and Juan Esteban Montero defeated former president Alessandri and took office in December 1931. Montero lasted in office only until June 1932, when a military-civilian *coup* led by Colonel Marmaduke Grove—one of the original leaders of the September 1924 military activities—took control, established a governing junta, dissolved congress, and proclaimed the "Socialist Republic of Chile."

The socialist republic lasted only twelve days, but some of the people who created it stayed in power until September 1932. They were generally quite progressive and instituted reforms that endured after they left office. A new military *coup* in September brought another change in government and finally the election of Arturo Alessandri to the presidency once again in 1932.

Alessandri won the presidency in 1932 as the candidate of the center parties. During his six-year term he remained in the center of the political spectrum, moving perhaps a bit to the right. He ran an unmitigatedly repressive presidential regime, but one which steered the country out of the disastrous depression and into an era of economic development.

Alessandri took office during the depths of the depression. Some 160,000 workers were unemployed in the capital. The national debt had reached towering proportions, and at a time when the national government could hope to deliver only minimal social services a typhoid epidemic was raging. The Lion of Tarapacá proved capable of meeting the awesome challenge facing him in 1932. Guided by his brilliant and bold financial advisor, Gustavo Ross, Alessandri directed a rise in exports from a value of 290 million pesos in 1932 to 948 million in 1937. Nitrate production rose to about 5 times what it had been when he took office. General industrial output increased markedly and unemployment was generally wiped out. Alessandri not only balanced his budget, in his last years he managed to produce a surplus. One of his most significant early acts was to dissolve COSACH and replace it in 1933 with the Chilean Nitrate and Iodine Corporation. The new company also had control over sales of the two products, but the government was legally assured of a say in its operations. Twenty-five percent of the company's profits were required to go to the national treasury.

With the economy revived, Alessandri was able to breathe life into already existing social security legislation. New programs were undertaken, medical and sanitation facilities improved. New schools were built, including agricultural and technical schools. But there was a price to pay for the improvements. Alessandri harassed his political opposition, both on the right and left of him. Relying especially on the internal security law passed during his term, he singled out Socialists and Communists for his oppression.

Again it appeared that an authoritarian regime could bring stability and economic development. But in fundamental ways the development did not improve the lot of the majority of Chileans. Basic inequalities continued to exist. The working class did not receive what one would think was its deserved share of the national income. Even worse, social reforms generally did not make their way into rural Chile. As part of the general economic program, the Alessandri administration had devalued the peso, and this contributed to an acute increase in the cost of living at a time when wages and salaries remained stable. By the time of the congressional elections of 1937, it was patently clear that the parties of the left were determined to elect their own candidate in the forthcoming presidential contest.

A Popular Front of leftist and center parties was formed for the congressional elections of 1937. Though it did not manage to gain control of the congress, it did well enough to encourage a concerted effort for the presidential election the following year. The Front got its start in 1936. Once the Soviet Comintern decided in 1935 that Communist parties should join with democratic and bourgeois parties in the fight against fascism, and Popular Front governments were established in Spain and France, it was likely that an attempt would be made to form one in Chile. The impetus for the creation of the Front in Chile, however, came from Radical party deputy Justiano Sotomayor.

The left wing of the Radical party found its opportunity to encourage the formation of a Popular Front in early 1936. On February 2 more than 10,000 railroad workers went on strike to secure wage increases that would keep pace with the rising cost of living. Workers in other industries soon went on sympathy strikes. On February 8 Alessandri declared the country in a state of siege, dissolved congress, and closed the opposition press. This was the rallying point around which the Front was formed. On March 26 a directorate representing Socialists (the party was formed in 1933), Communists, Radicals, Democrats, Democrat-Socialists, and others was organized. Shortly the directorate announced a three-point overall program of action:

1. Against oppression and in favor of the restoration of the democratic liberties

2. Against imperialism and for the achievement of Chile for the Chileans

3. Against the material and intellectual misery of the people and for the realization of a modern socioeconomic justice for the middle and working classes.[2]

The Popular Front represented both the middle class and the proletariat. For the first time these groups joined together in a formal and highly organized effort to defeat the rightist parties, especially the Conservatives and the Liberals. The power brokers of the left and center parties were not merely being expedient in forming the Front; they were drawn together also by manifest ideological preferences. The issues separating the Front from the rightist parties in the presidential election of 1938 were substantive.

The Front ran a moderate Radical, Pedro Aguirre Cerda, as its candidate against Gustavo Ross. Aguirre had come from the most modest background and had worked his way through school, earning degrees in education and law. A deputy, minister, and then senator, Aguirre had acquired considerable wealth and finally a famous fundo. The Front's extensive platform was brought home to the masses with the slogan: *Pan, techo y abrigo* (Bread, roof, and overcoat). Campaigning throughout the country, attended by supporters of proven political appeal, Aguirre won the election by some 4,000 votes out of the nearly 500,000 cast.

Considering the disparate interests and traditional antagonisms within the center and left parties, it is remarkable that the Popular Front had enough cohesion to elect a president. With the election won, the Front managed to maintain its unity only briefly. The Socialist party withdrew in 1940, and the Popular Front broke up formally the following year. Yet coalitions of center and left parties continued to hold power through the 1940s. President Aguirre was forced to resign in November 1941 because of his poor health, and he died shortly thereafter. Aguirre was followed in office by another moderate Radical, Juan Antonio Ríos, who governed until he died in 1946.

The Popular Front, like so many reformist regimes before it,

---

[2] Cited in John Reese Stevenson, *The Chilean Popular Front* (Philadelphia, 1942), p. 71.

failed to redeem even a fraction of its campaign pledges. Working against its success was a congress controlled by the opposition. But even within the Front itself there were many influential moderates who were dedicated essentially to the reform and development of the existing socioeconomic system; they were not disposed to overturn it.

There was, in fact, striking progress during the Front's three years. Two months after the Front took control of the government a ruinous earthquake struck the south and took some 50,000 lives and injured and left homeless a greater number. The shocking devastation both reduced the Front's potential for immediate reform and yet made possible the creation of a vehicle to carry out the promised economic development. The Chilean Development Corporation (CORFO) was chartered and funded to supervise the country's economic development as a whole. In the face of the earthquake and the obvious need to coordinate resources and efforts, many conservative members of congress who might ordinarily have been against such a powerful corporation supported its creation. CORFO was given the responsibility of increasing industrial production, balancing international trade, improving agricultural productivity, attracting local private capital to industry, and raising the general standard of living.

In its short term of office the Popular Front was able to increase industrial productivity, aid in the mechanization of agriculture, raise wages, and protect working-class rights. These were impressive gains, but they did not indicate a fundamental change in the socioeconomic system.

The presidential election of 1946 was won by another Radical, Gabriel González Videla, but he did not gain an absolute majority. The election, therefore, had to be decided in congress. González's ultimate election was accomplished with the support of the Liberals in congress. The multiparty nature of Chilean politics in the twentieth century and a president's dependence on more than one of them for power was demonstrated vividly in González's first cabinet. It was composed of three Radicals, three Liberals, and three Communists. This was indeed a strange coalition. Shortly the Liberals left the administration and the president fired the Communists. González then formed a Radical government. In 1948 he secured a law that made the Communist party illegal. It remained illegal until 1958.

Ex-dictator Ibáñez, speaking of reform and considering himself above sordid politics, won the presidential election of 1952. By the end of his administration he was indeed above politics, for he had lost his political support and his general popularity. It had appeared to people of all social strata that Ibáñez was the man capable of leading the country out of the doldrums seemingly created by previous mediocre administrations and the man to restore honesty to government. In both respects he failed his supporters. The basic problems of inflation, latifundism, foreign control of the copper industry (now the leading export mineral), and the pressing need for further social reform persisted and troubled a growing number of Chileans. Nor did Ibáñez bring honesty to government.

There were several consequential developments during the Ibáñez administration, however. Shortly before the presidential election of 1958 the Communist party was legalized. Electoral reform laws were passed which lessened the possibility of vote purchasing and gave the lower classes a more effective franchise. The Christian Democratic party (PDC), a center-left party made up of the old *Falange Nacional* and members of the Conservative party, was formed. It would elect Eduardo Frei to the presidency in 1964. A coalition of left parties, called the Popular Action Front (FRAP), was also formed during the Ibáñez administration. An expanded version would elect Salvador Allende to the presidency in 1970.

The Ibáñez administration also helped enliven the Chilean labor movement, although perhaps not in the manner it intended. The new administration was determined to gain control of the labor movement; it even sponsored new unions. However, the more powerful labor leaders were fearful of the administration's intentions, and they responded by forming a new and more effective overall union, the *Central Unica de Trabajadores de Chile* (CUTCH).

The presidential election of 1958 was won by Jorge Alessandri, son of the former president, with the support of the Conservatives and Liberals. He beat both Frei and Allende, but it was the last victory for the parties of the right, the last time that a candidate with traditional goals and methods would win, at least for the moment. Alessandri was an enormously popular figure, but he was not able to cope with the needs of the Chilean populace or its economy. And this was at a time when the Christian Democratic party and the FRAP were calling for fundamental change.

Promising a "Revolution in Liberty" Eduardo Frei won the presidential election of 1964. The Christian Democrats pledged themselves to revolutionary socioeconomic change within the context of democracy. Clearly they aroused more hopes than they satisfied since they were defeated in 1970 when Chile elected Marxist-Socialist Salvador Allende to the presidency. Before looking at these two critical presidencies it is worthwhile to examine some of the central problems faced by previous Chilean administrations, problems which contributed to the elections first of Frei and then of Allende.

It should not be surprising that Chile elected first a center-left Christian Democrat to the presidency and then an avowed Marxist. It is overwhelmingly clear that during the twentieth century Chile has witnessed great extremes of prosperity and poverty, with the preponderant majority of the country's population neither sharing in the prosperity nor possessing the optimism that wealth was there for the taking merely if one would apply himself industriously, an optimism necessary for the smooth functioning of capitalism in the era of mass democracy, an optimism that had been so prevalent during the nineteenth century. It has been estimated that in 1943, 77 percent of the Chilean work force did not earn enough to support in decency a family of four. These figures are shocking enough, but there are further complicating factors. In 1946, 4.3 percent of government revenues derived from direct taxes, but in 1952 this was down to 4 percent. During the same period income from indirect taxes increased from 7.8 percent to 9.2 percent of the total. As is well known, indirect taxes bear more heavily on the poor than the rich. Between 1940 and 1950 government income from internal taxation, that is, not counting customs revenue, amounted only to between about 13 and 16 percent of the total. To make matters worse, it was estimated in 1956 that the country's rich were paying 14.7 percent of their income in taxes and were spending 64.3 percent of their income on consumer goods. Thus for a long time it appeared to many Chileans that a more equitable system of taxation would not only lessen poverty directly, it would make capital available for the country's economic development. It is quite fantastic, but during the late 1950s the government in its effort to fight inflation proposed that the workers bear the brunt of the fight by accepting wage readjustments of only one-third of the increase in the cost of living. This policy was suggested by North American advisors in the private Klein-Saks mission.[3]

Many people in the United States are only now coming to recognize the corrosive and demoralizing effects of a spiralling inflation. And in the United States we are speaking of a wild inflation of about 6 percent per year. Using 1940 as a starting point, with a cost of living index of 100, the Chilean inflation was so great that in 1945 the index was 204.6; in 1950, 511, in 1955, 2,887. Chile's cost of living index rose 56 percent in 1953, 70 percent the following year, 80 percent in 1955, and 40 percent in 1956. (Based on official prices the cost of living rose approximately 100 percent during the first 9 months of 1972.)

New tax legislation notwithstanding, the relative position of the low-income groups has decreased during the last decades. The Chilean Development Corporation has estimated that between 1940 and 1953 the real income of all groups increased about 40 percent. However, manual workers, who comprised about 57 percent of the total work force, saw their real income increase by only 7 percent. Yet at the same time the real income of white-collar workers increased about 46 percent and that of proprietors, the self-employed, and workers in the service industries increased by

[3] The Klein-Saks mission was brought to Chile in 1955 to recommend an anti-inflation program. The mission had earlier had some success in fighting inflation in Peru.

about 60 percent. Thus there was a regressive redistribution of total income that favored the middle class more than any other. This alteration occurred at the expense of the working classes rather than the rich. From the workers' point of view there was neither prosperity nor the illusion of it. Under such circumstances it is difficult for capitalism to exist. The inflationary spiral even vitiated the healthy growth of the middle class by making it difficult and at times impossible to accumulate capital and thereby proceed upward on the socioeconomic ladder. A great many members of the middle class, including small industrialists, favored controls in the economy, such as wage-price and credit controls. They also lost faith in the market economy.

Taxation and inflation were not the only problems that contrived to render capitalism less than appealing to many Chileans. Chileans, as well as citizens of many another underdeveloped country, have long recognized that their capitalism was not the open, competitive brand of Smithian lore, but the closed, noncompetitive monopoly capitalism that has often been the reality of the modern variety even in developed countries. A 1961 Chilean study demonstrated poignantly that agriculture, mining, industry, and services were controlled by a very small percentage of the population. In many cases one or two banking groups and families controlled—and continued to control until after the election of Salvador Allende—an industry. These were demoralizing facts for Chileans. So many people have not partaken of the country's wealth and prosperity that such information about the monopolistic nature of their economy tends to be terribly depressing and tends to create revolutionaries.

There was also the problem of the welfare state. Chile has built one of the most advanced systems of social services in the world. Practically everyone has become dependent on it to one degree or another. With the inflation wiping out personal savings within the middle class, even it became dependent on such social services as health, accident and unemployment benefits, and pensions. So great have the benefits been, and so easy has it been to retire at attractive stipends that the government could hardly afford to support the system without further contributing to the inflation. The advanced welfare system fired the inflation and made increased benefits necessary. This in turn spurred the inflation.

A rapidly rising population and urban growth has made it impossible for the government to deliver basic services such as housing and education. In 1940 Chile had a population of 5,023,500, including an urban population of 2,637,300; in 1960 the total population was 7,375,200, including an urban population of 4,902,500. The percentage of rural population declined during the two decades from 47.5 percent to 33.5 percent. In 1961 the government estimated that the country needed 550,000 housing units. (The destructive earthquakes of 1960 contributed to this number.) The government expected this shortage to increase by some 38,000 units a year. During the 1960s the government could not keep pace with the mounting deficit, and even when progress was made it was generally not the very lowest income groups who benefited. Thus Chile has its *poblaciones callampas,* its mushroom towns, immense slums of improvised shacks that have sprung up around the major urban centers, especially Santiago. Perhaps a half million people live in the callampas that surround Santiago. The callampas have been breeding grounds for radical sentiment.

The rising population has also made it impossible for the government to keep up with educational facilities. The government has invested heavily in public education, but mostly in urban areas. It was estimated in 1960 that 27.5 percent of working-class children drop out of school after only 1 year, that 50 percent do not complete 3 years of schooling and that 85 percent terminate their education after 6 years. Such sad figures suggest the further stratification of Chilean society and the lack of opportunity facing the proletarian youth. Though Chile has one of the highest official literacy rates in the world, one must question the level of comprehension of sophisticated issues among the masses.

Of all the problems that have undermined Chilean development and brought enough people to the far left so that first a Christian Democrat could be elected president and then a Marxist, the two most spectacular have been neocolonialism and the so-called neofeudal landholding system.

Chileans do not consider the copper industry the only example of neocolonialism in their country. There is another more subtle but equally dispiriting form of neocolonialism in the Chilean economy that has created a dependence on foreigners. During the nineteenth and early twentieth centuries underdeveloped countries like Chile were able to import modern technology that was fairly inexpensive and long-lived. Thus a steam engine, railroad, or steel plant could be purchased abroad, sometimes secondhand, and used in the underdeveloped country for many years, even decades; but the modern technology of the post–World War II period is immeasurably more sophisticated and short-lived. Consequently, the underdeveloped country becomes dependent on the developed country for its technology, that is, the machinery of modern business and industry. Not only have the underdeveloped countries become dependent on the constant supply of foreign technology for their continued economic expansion, these modern and highly technological improvements have shown themselves to be capital-intensive and not labor-intensive. That is, they cost a great deal of money, and they create few jobs and often eliminate many jobs. This is a very awkward situation for an underdeveloped country with a large semiskilled labor force.

But what is probably more troublesome, a phenomenon that shocked many Chileans as they became aware of it, is the problem of deficit capital investment. North Americans often are eager to believe that they are doing a considerable service by investing great sums of capital in underdeveloped countries (countries that clearly need and usually want development capital), that this capital is productive, and that the investors are entitled to a fair share of the profits. What they do not appear to realize is that, as has been demonstrated especially during the last decade, the foreign companies often take out of the underdeveloped country more money than they ever put in. Because of the many available methods of bookkeeping, it is just not possible to determine accurately the rate of profit for North American companies operating in Chile. One credible estimate is that all United States investments in Chile in 1969 produced a return of 17.4 percent. In 1967 the copper industry was supposed to have produced a return on invested capital of

27.3 percent. These figures may be a bit high (although when they are based on the re-use of depreciated equipment, as is sometimes the case, the figures may even be low), but they would not seem so to many Chileans. President Allende argues that in the last four decades or so the foreign copper mine owners have taken out of Chile some $3 billion on an initial investment of $10 million. Although these figures are grossly inaccurate (for instance, the Guggenheims purchased control of Chuquicamata for about $25 million, and another $100 million was spent in making the mine profitable), no doubt many Chileans believe them. Allende has observed that during the course of the present century about 10 billion dollars have been taken out of Chile, that is, an amount equal to all the capital accumulated in Chile over four centuries. Taking the 17.4 and 27.3 percent figures, we see that it would take a North American company 4 to 6 years to recoup its investment and another 4 to 6 to make 100 percent profit. That is, after 8 to 12 years the foreign company is a net exporter of capital from Chile. And this occurs in a country that sorely needs capital. Even when the foreign company increases its investment by replacing equipment and expanding facilities, it is still surely to be an exporter of capital. The problem is exacerbated when the foreign company borrows money from public and private sources within the underdeveloped country. Chile has also become aware of the fact that foreigners at times establish companies with old and obsolete equipment that no longer serves well in the developed country and then depreciate it once again.

Another subtle form of neocolonialism is the international loan, especially as offered by the United States. The United States government has loaned Chile impressive amounts of capital designed to favor well-regarded administrations such as Frei's. (That is, Frei as opposed to someone like Allende. Allende has gotten little from the United States but a cold shoulder. Chile could not even get a loan to purchase three additional Boeing jets. If Chile has to turn to the Soviet bloc, it will have to outlay exceedingly large and unnecessary amounts of capital to revamp its training of pilots and to change its spare parts and service systems.) But the loans from the United States or its dependent international agencies are often tied to the purchase of United States goods. Because of their price this has raised costs considerably—and helped spur the inflation—and left Chile dependent on the United States for a continuous supply of spare parts. Finally, Chile's foreign debt is so great that service costs are a constant and weighty factor in the incessant inflation. The country's debt nearly doubled between 1958 and 1961 alone, going from $569 million to $1 billion.

It is apparent that if the United States desires to sponsor economic expansion in the underdeveloped countries, it will have to design more equitable means of loaning capital than it has in the past.

Copper is Chile's major economic resource. It provides the single largest source of foreign exchange and it accounts for a sizable percentage of government revenues. The Gran Minería, owned by United States interests, turned out about 85 percent of the total copper production in the recent past. We have already seen how the foreigners gained virtual domination of the copper industry. What was not mentioned is that during the early twentieth century Chileans themselves had enough capital to assume control of the leading mines had they so desired. Chilean capital was then invested in large quantity in Bolivian tin mining operations, in northern Chilean nitrates, and in Argentine beef production. The large copper ventures were slow to return profits and the Chileans preferred to invest in more lucrative businesses. This attitude on the part of the Chileans was one of the central reasons for the denationalization of the copper industry.

Until 1925 the copper industry was lightly taxed. It was only then that the Chilean government began to tax it seriously. Direct taxes on profits were raised to 12 percent. Nitrate revenues were declining during the 1920s, and the government needed another source of income, so it increased its taxes on the copper industry, both foreign and domestically owned. During the 1930s the direct tax was increased to 18 percent, and exchange controls amounted to an additional indirect tax. In 1939 the Popular Front established the Chilean Development Corporation to preside over national economic development. To fund CORFO the government decided to raise the tax on copper production. The tax on profits, therefore, was raised from 18 to 33 percent. With such a tax structure the Gran Minería could no longer earn as much as Chilean industrial corporations. Taxes went even higher in the 1950s. In 1953 the direct tax rate on copper profits was 60 percent. Chile was no longer employing copper taxes essentially to sponsor the country's economic development, it was now using such revenue for current operating expenses also. However, the "New Deal" copper law of 1955 reduced the direct tax to 50 percent and added additional taxes that would decline as production rose. The new policy stimulated increased investment on the part of the copper companies.

By the early 1960s copper was a highly politicized and emotional issue. Practically all of the country's problems were blamed on the foreign ownership of the industry and the remittance of profits abroad. The issue contributed mightily to the election of the center-left Christian Democratic administration in 1964 and then finally to the election of Allende in 1970. We shall examine the copper programs of both Frei and Allende momentarily.

The supposedly neofeudal landholding system is the second of the two problems that more than any others have led to the elections of Frei and Allende. We have already seen that Chilean agriculture has been by and large capitalist with some neofeudal holdovers. In fact, large landholdings are very much a part of the capitalist system. But the issue of large estates and peasant exploitation has become so politicized and emotional that any progressive party would have to promise extensive reform to get elected to office.

All throughout Chilean history there has been an argument over whether the country is a rich or poor one. Some Chileans have always maintained that the country is rich, that it has the natural resources to support its population in conspicuous prosperity, while others have argued that the country is intrinsically poor. Without entering this argument, it seems safe to conclude that Chile has the land and climate to supply its own agricultural needs either directly through production or indirectly through barter of agricultural goods on the international market.

A 1956 study estimated that only 20 percent of Chile's land area was then being devoted to agriculture. Of this figure a full 46 percent was devoted to natural pastures or to cultivated land left out of production. This means that practically the entire agricultural population was being confined to the remaining 54 percent, approximately 10 percent of Chile's land area. (In the 1960s about 30 percent of Chile's active population depended directly on the land for their living, but they produced only about 12 percent of the gross national product.) To make matters worse, it is known that proper crop rotation will improve land better than the old system of leaving land at rest in the form of natural pasture. And it has been demonstrated that cattle do much better on land cultivated artificially, through seeding, than on natural pasturage. In 1956 most of the country's agricultural land was being devoted to cereal and meat production, surely not the best way to get the most return per unit of land.

To appreciate the complexities of the agricultural situation over the past few decades, one must bear in mind that there has been an ineffable general lack of prosperity or economic optimism in Chile and that a majority of the rural population has owned too little to earn a decent living while an extreme minority of that population has owned more land than they have been willing to cultivate.[4] According to 1930 figures, holdings of 1,000 or more hectares (2.47 acres to an hectare) comprised 78 percent of the country's cultivable land. But the number of these farms comprised only 2 percent of the country's total. Holdings of between 50 and 1,000 hectares accounted for 18 percent of the total cultivable area and

---

[4] For instance, a 1960 study of rural poverty estimated that 37 percent of the houses of inquilinos (generally those farmworkers who held land in return for labor services on the owner's property) in the region of San Vicente de Tagua Tagua in O'Higgins province had only dirt floors. Sixty percent of their houses lacked all sanitary facilities. In 57 percent of the houses water for daily use was taken from open canals or ditches. Yet, the position of the inquilino was usually not as bad as that of landless farmworkers, especially day laborers and migrants. It was also estimated that if the inquilinos spent between 70 and 80 percent of their income on food, they could not provide themselves and their families with a minimally acceptable standard of nutrition.

comprised 16 percent of the total farms. But those of between 5 and 50 hectares covered only 4 percent of the total cultivable land, while comprising 82 percent of the total number of farms. According to the 1955 agricultural census 9.7 percent of the farms comprised 86 percent of the country's total cultivable land. Farms of between 1 and 49 hectares, representing 74.6 percent of the total number of farms, comprised only 5.2 percent of the cultivable land. In the important agricultural provinces of Santiago, Valparaíso, and Aconcagua, 7 percent of the farms covered 92 percent of the cultivable land, while 84.8 percent of the farms covered only 3.2 percent of the cultivable land. During the 1950s, 1 percent of those actively engaged in agriculture received 25 percent of the annual income produced in this sector of the economy. In a country with so little general prosperity and so much general poverty there should be little wonder that the landholding situation became a preeminent political issue.

There is an interesting and quite cheerless sidelight to the agricultural situation. Small landowners have had a more difficult time obtaining credit than large landowners. To increase the chance of a loan the small owners have tended to raise their own evaluations of the net worth of their farms above what a large owner would be inclined to do. Not only have they received less credit, but as a result of their own higher evaluations they have had to pay relatively higher taxes than the large owners.

And it has been shown that small farms in Chile have a tendency to be more productive than large farms. This phenomenon has been studied in a small, highly agricultural region near Santiago. The government began a program of land reform there in 1929. The previous year there had been 67 parcels of land. In 1954 there were 330 parcels covering the same land area. Thus, nearly 60 percent of the land had undergone some form of subdivision during the period. In 1896 the area contained only 49 properties, of which only 3 were less than 100 hectares. In 1928, of the 67 properties only 10 were less than 100 hectares. But in 1954, of the 330 properties fully 86 percent were less than 100 hectares and 61 percent were less than 25 hectares. This significant change in the nature of the region's land holding was induced partly by direct government intervention and partly by the natural consequences of a market economy. By 1954 most of the region's landowners lived in Santiago and not on the farms. Most of them were from the rising middle class, and many of these invested in land as a hedge against the spiralling inflation. The most unstable parcels were those of 25 hectares or less; these changed hands the most frequently. The smaller farms altered the region's traditional pattern of agricultural productivity. Where the region traditionally, that is, when most farms were large ones, devoted its land to cereals and pasturage, the small farms were devoting their land to fruits, vineyards, and more recently aviculture. The larger farms have become more involved in milk production and have mechanized quite extensively. There has even been more diversification in crop production, but the large farms continued to use most of their land for the growing of forage, especially alfalfa and clover, and cereals. This is extensive, low-intensity production. The small farms were much more intensively cultivated and, therefore, had a higher rate of productivity.

This is one of the things Chileans have in mind when they speak of their neofeudal agriculture. It would probably be preferable from an academic standpoint if they referred to the situation of rural poverty among the masses at a time when an enormous amount of land is either not being used or is not being used as productively as it might be as underdeveloped capitalism or poor or bad capitalism, but from a social point of view the term "neofeudal" is quite instructive. According to a United Nations study in 1953, 22 percent of the irrigated area of large farms in the provinces of Santiago and Valparaíso was devoted to natural pastures although this land was entirely suited to intensive farming operations. And it appears that a rather high percentage of the large owners were not interested in changing the situation. There can be little doubt that if the large farms throughout Chile, and certainly the irrigated regions, had devoted themselves to high-intensity production rather than cereals and pasturage with nearly half their land not producing anything socially valuable in the short run, the agricultural issue would never have been able to become quite the political issue it finally did.

Agricultural productivity clearly has not kept pace with the increasing demands of an expanding society. In the years just prior to 1960 the population was rising by over 2 percent annually but agricultural production was rising by only 1.4 percent. Chile was now an importer of basic foodstuffs. Currency that could have been used to purchase capital goods had to be used for imported agricultural products, including meat. Instead of earning additional foreign currency by exporting these agricultural products or at least by not having to import them, the country was forced to borrow internationally to aid its economic development. This in turn fired the inflation.

But the agricultural situation prior to the presidential election of 1964 was not due entirely to the attitudes and practices of the large landowners. The plight of agriculture has been due in great part also to the emphasis the government has placed on industrial development. During the 1930s the government chose to protect industry through various indirect methods, such as tariffs. It was the Popular Front government that first rhapsodized industry and shifted government attention overwhelmingly in its favor. Industrialization has become intertwined with nationalism. Chileans saw in industrialization a means of lessening dependence on the foreign powers, a means of providing jobs for the urban masses, and a means also of breaking the power of the landed rich. Actually, industrialization did not live up to its advance billing in any of the three areas, although Chile has become one of Spanish America's most industrialized countries. Some ideologues favored industrialization because it promised to proletarianize the supposedly semi-feudal society and bring the country that much closer to the eventual class war. The large landowners generally went along with the drive for industrialization partly because many of them were related through financial or familial ties to industry or big business, partly because industrialization did not threaten the breakup of their estates, and partly because the landed rich were not as powerful in the industrial period as tradition would have it, and they could do little about the new emphasis.

The Popular Front established CORFO to carry out economic development. It was paid for by mining taxes and it concentrated on industry to the decided disadvantage of agriculture. Until 1964 only a very small percentage of CORFO's credits and investments were directed to agriculture. Agriculture stagnated to a large extent because the government refused to finance land reform and because it undermined agricultural productivity by imposing price controls on a wide variety of products and subsidized imported agricultural products. Such a governmental posture has frustrated agricultural incentive. In the several cases in which the government protected and otherwise helped the cultivation of certain products, such as wheat and sunflower, production rose markedly. The Chilean agricultural community has responded readily to the possibility of financial reward. There has not always been such incentive, and real profits, according to CORFO, were negative in five out of thirteen years between 1940 and 1952. One wonders what the nature of agricultural productivity would be were that sector of the economy treated to the protection and attention received by industry over the past several decades.

Yet the picture of agricultural productivity remains supremely complex. For instance, although price controls certainly have limited productivity since the Second World War by making extra production less attractive, agricultural prices have risen more than any other group. Starting with a 1947 base of 100, prices in 1954 were: agricultural, 559; industrial, 447; mineral, 549; imports, 447; general, 481. And while landowners have rightly noted that they have not been making more than a modest income on capital invested, they at times have charged spectacularly for lands rented to peasants. It is also true that the landowners have been taxed proportionally less than other sectors of the economy.

Yet Chileans have been faced with the ultimate fact that there has been underutilization of land, underproductivity, and hundreds of thousands of peasants who have not been earning enough to support themselves decently and who have not added to an internal market that would further promote industrialization. The problem has been dramatically politicized by the rise of a modern, capitalistic, rural proletariat. There was already a significant switch to wage labor among rural workers in central Chile during the late nineteenth century and, therefore, a breakdown of the traditional system of inquilinaje. The change-over to wage labor recently has ended many of the former neofeudal relations between worker and owner, including the worker's sense of security. In the agricultural region near Santiago mentioned earlier it was found that as the size of the farm decreased, so too did the traditional forms of inquilinaje. By the time we get to the farms of 25 hectares or less the workers are almost exclusively salaried. The salaried workers have lost their sense of security and, along with it, their loyalty to the owners. The constant change of ownership, especially of the small farms, has contributed both to the loss of security and the absence of loyalty. This phenomenon has become quite generalized throughout Chile, although it has been most intense in the central region. The result has been the enormous rise in rural unionism, rural strikes (three times the number of peasants took part in strikes in 1965 as did in the previous year), and finally the political drive to break up the large estates.

These are some of the problems and issues that made the election of Salvador Allende, a Marxist senator with a medical degree, and a member of the Socialist party (which in Chile is further to the left than the Communist party), if not inevitable, at least not remarkable. The two previous administrations did much to pave the way for his election. Alessandri was committed to orthodox means in the effort to halt the inflation and secure monetary stability. Thus he relied on traditional price and wage controls to a great extent. But he also introduced certain reforms that, without tampering very much with the fundamental social structure, managed to raise hopes and make formerly radical positions seem less so.

Alessandri both introduced a broad tax reform in the early 1960s and turned his attention to agriculture. The original agency of land reform, the *Caja de Colonización* (the Colonization Office) had been established in 1928. In three decades it had redistributed notoriously little land and created few new farm units. The Caja was reorganized somewhat in 1960 and the pace of land reform quickened noticeably. In 1962 the Agrarian Reform Law was passed, which created the Agrarian Reform Corporation, CORA. Land reform had moved into its serious stage. CORA was authorized to expropriate land under a large category of circumstances. Thus it could expropriate land not being used or land being underutilized. All land expropriated had to be paid for in full at the time of expropriation. A constitutional amendment the following year permitted payment of only 10 percent of value at the time of expropriation with further payments spread over a period of years for certain categories of land.

The government now had the machinery to undertake a far-reaching land reform. But from the standpoint of the left it got off to a disappointingly slow start. From its creation in November 1962 until the end of August 1963 CORA had expropriated only 11 farms comprising some 61,620 hectares.

The Alessandri administration served as a transition period in which serious reforms were undertaken and formerly radical positions were sponsored in the most respectable circles. The way was being cleared for the elections of Frei and Allende, although many people supported reforms precisely to avert such an eventuality. Two additional factors contributed to this denouement. One is that the church had become an active supporter of reform. It not only inspired reform, it contributed to its respectability. The other is the electoral reforms carried out in 1949 (the enfranchisement of women), 1958, and 1962. Taken together these reforms increased the number of registered voters spectacularly and made it less possible for the upper classes to control the votes of the lower middle class and the proletariat. Added to this was the legalization of the Communist party in 1958.

As the presidential election of 1964 approached, it became manifestly clear that the population was moving far to the left in the political spectrum. The candidate of the extreme left was Salvador Allende, supported by the FRAP. Eduardo Frei, the Christian Democratic candidate, was somewhere between center and left. The candidate of the right was Julio Durán, supported by the Democratic Front. When it became evident that in such a race Allende would win, the Conservatives and Liberals threw their weight in favor of Frei. Members of the Radical party were to be found in all three camps. As it turned out Frei received 56.1 percent of the vote, Allende, 38.9 percent, and Durán only 5 percent.

Through the ballot box Frei had brought his revolution in liberty home to the people. But he promised great things, significantly more than he could deliver. Like Marxism, Christian democracy means different things to different people, including its own adherents. It speaks of humanitarianism and a "communitarian society." It purports to be a third position, somewhere between Marxism and capitalism. It is concerned with the individual and his loss of dignity through the industrial process and places emphasis on the concept of community rather than the isolated and competitive individual. Underpinning Christian democracy's ideological bent is the belief in Christian values, something which brought the PDC the indirect support of the Catholic church and the direct support of the female vote. Frei received 50 percent of the male vote and 63 percent of the female vote. Allende received 45 percent of the male vote and only 32 percent of the female vote.

Frei determined to regenerate society through two basic reforms. Through additional controls on the copper industry he expected to increase production and therefore state revenues, a necessary first step in any dedicated reform program. Second, he proposed a fundamental land reform, concentrating initially on rural unionization, raising rural wages, and a more efficient and equitable rural taxation system. His immediate goal was to raise rural wages and increase agricultural productivity. Eventually, the peasants were to become the owners of the land they worked. Neither of these two basic reforms was a profound threat to the right in the immediate future. The program did not envision wholesale land expropriation or nationalization of the copper industry.

Frei's agrarian program did not live up to its expectations. While rural wages were raised, inflation continued and wiped out gains, and the country still had to import basic foodstuffs. Frei had promised to redistribute land to 100,000 peasant families by 1970. This ambitious figure was later revised down to between 40,000 and 60,000 families. By June 1968 CORA had expropriated only 655 farms, covering an area of 1.25 million hectares. Fewer than 10,500 families had been given land. Even with these modest figures, which were so dismal to the peasantry, the actual situation was worse. Much of the land expropriated was public land, and little of it was irrigated. To complicate matters the government did not support the new landholding peasant families with sufficient credit and technical assistance. Yet the Frei administration, over rightist opposition, did pass a fundamental land reform act, one of the world's most progressive, in July 1967. The government was authorized to expropriate all landholdings of more than 80 hectares in the fertile central region or its equivalent elsewhere. By the time his term expired in 1970 Frei had only taken limited advantage of the new law.

In 1965 Frei's copper bill, designed to Chileanize the copper industry, was passed by congress. The FRAP had fought for outright nationalization. The new copper bill guaranteed that there would be no nationalization. The North American companies promised to increase production and to refine more copper in Chile. The law permitted the Chilean government to purchase 51 percent of the stock of the El Teniente mine and to receive 25 percent of the stock in two new companies called Cerro Exploration and Exótica. The government was also to be given 33 percent of the stock of any new companies formed by Anaconda. Further investment by both the Chilean government and the companies was supposed to double production by 1970.

The Chileanization of the copper industry was a great disappointment to the far left. In return for increased investment (which for Braden meant the reinvestment of funds received from the Chilean government for the 51 percent ownership of El Teniente), the government lowered taxes on copper production. Nor were all labor groups happy. In January 1966 the El Teniente mine workers struck for higher wages. A sympathy strike eventually ensued in other mines in the north and in March the government sent in troops. Attacking a union building at the El Salvador mine, the troops killed six men and two women.

Although Frei was comparatively successful in stemming the

inflation, it still managed to rise substantially—by 25.9 percent in 1965, 17 percent in 1966, and 24 percent in 1967. It was unduly high also in the final years of his administration. Initially, Frei attacked inflation from a "structuralist" position, believing that inflation should be decreased slowly through basic economic development rather than through monetary controls.[5] However, he eventually moved in the direction of monetary controls.

Frei also could not keep pace with the growing demand for housing and education facilities. Chile needed 600,000 housing units in 1964. Frei promised to build 360,000 new units in 6 years. After a strong beginning the housing effort faltered. With a rate of population growth of 2.5 percent per year, Frei could barely keep pace with additional requirements much less make inroads on the deficit. Equally nettlesome was education. Frei built thousands of schools, and government expenditures on education increased by 66 percent between 1964 and 1967. Yet most of the money had to be used for structures rather than improving the quality of education. Expenditures by the government for health services rose by 50 percent during the same 3 years. But all in all a good many Chileans wanted more of everything.

By 1970 the rising inflation, wage and salary controls, rising taxes, a frequent shortage of consumer goods, and the nationalistic issue of who should own the copper industry had threatened the basis of the PDC's urban support and forced key elements within the party to the far left. In the presidential election of 1970 the positions of Allende and Radomiro Tomic, the PDC candidate, were only moderately different.

Eduardo Frei treated Chile to one of the most radical and progressive governments in the history of Latin America. Frei was a personally popular figure, and had he been able to succeed himself, there is little likelihood that he would have been defeated. But without that possibility the Christian Democrats chose

[5] For instance, structuralists generally advocate placing immediate attention on agrarian reform and lessening the country's dependence on the vagaries of foreign trade.

Radomiro Tomic as their candidate. Tomic took the party directly into the far left. He called for total nationalization of the copper industry. The right organized itself tightly around the National party and former president Jorge Alessandri. A third party or coalition, *Unidad Popular* (UP), brought together the winning combination of left parties and even the large and important Radical party. In addition to the Radicals, the UP contained the Communists and Allende's Socialists, among others. Allende received only a slight plurality of about 36 percent of the popular vote. Alessandri received some 35 percent, and Tomic, only 28 percent. The election was thrown into congress, which after a period of feverish speculation selected Allende as president.

Allende wasted little time in implementing his program. Wages were raised and prices held. Inflation was held to only 7.5 percent during the first five months of 1971, compared with 22 percent during the same period the previous year. By mid-1971 there had generally been a 40 percent increase in real wages. There was such an increased demand for consumer goods that Chilean factories were working at full capacity for the first time in years. There were no more games to be played about nationalization. Within nine months of his taking office in November 1970, most of the country's textile, iron, automobile assembly, and copper industries belonged to the government. One of the central concerns of the left has been state control of credit. Whoever controls credit can control developmental priorities and development itself. Within a short while after taking office Allende had taken control of some 60 percent of the country's banking institutions.

Nationalization of the copper industry and expropriation of great amounts of land have been the hallmarks of the Allende administration. In July 1971 the government nationalized the holdings of the three largest copper companies in Chile: Cerro, Anaconda, and Kennecott. During its first six months in office the administration expropriated nearly a million and a half hectares of land.

There is no mistaking Allende's intent and direction. Whether or not he will be able to carry out his revolution through constitutional means is difficult to tell at this writing. The government's overall policy of reform has generated further inflation. In one short period in 1972 prices rose by 90 percent on cotton goods, 70 percent on wine, 110 percent on cigarettes, 90 percent on milk, 100 percent on sugar, 100 percent on chicken and 110 percent on automobile parts.[6] For the year 1972, as a whole, inflation increased more than 160 percent, making it the highest in the world. To complicate the situation, industrial production has been unable to keep pace with demand and there is a critical shortage of consumer goods once more. The land reform program is not proceeding as fast as some of Allende's influential supporters demand. Copper production has fallen and gold reserves have dwindled. There is not enough housing. A nationwide strike of several weeks duration caused Allende to declare a state of siege in many parts of the country and finally to reshuffle his cabinet, appointing two generals and an admiral to ministerial posts, including an army commander, General Arturo Prats, to the crucial and sensitive post of minister of interior. Yet in the important congressional elections of March 4, 1973, Allende's coalition actually increased its popular vote a few percentage points over that which it received in the 1970 presidential elections. The UP even gained a few seats in the congress, although it is still in the minority in both houses, something which will continue to make it difficult for the president to achieve his goals.

One of the bright spots is the potential of the Andean Common Market, established in 1969, which includes Chile, Bolivia, Colombia, Ecuador, and Peru. In three years trade among the Andean group has doubled. In 1972 the five countries reached an agreement for coordinated production of industrial commodities, including an international division of production responsibility. If nationalism remains subordinate to the needs of the group as a whole, the prospects seem unlimited.

The old capitalism is no longer at issue in Chile; it has failed to satisfy the requirements of a majority of the people. There are two fundamental questions to be answered now. One is whether constitutional government will continue to function in Chile. The broad

6 *New York Times,* September 3, 1972.

middle class obviously requires private property rights and the profit motive to function. Though many members of the middle class, especially of the lower middle class, voted for Allende—doubtless in great part because of his strong anti-imperialist stand—the Chilean middle class has not wanted the destruction of the basic capitalist system. It is apparent now that even members of the lower middle class, especially the small shopkeepers, are disenchanted with the extent of Allende's reforms. Booting the foreign colonialists out and sharing the wealth is one thing, but threatening the right to be in business and make profits is quite another.

The other question is where political power is to reside ultimately, with the individual or with society at large. If it is to be the individual, then Chile will continue to have its traditional political liberalism or democracy; if it is to be society at large, as a good many of Allende's partisans would have it, then Chile will likely have a dictatorship of the proletariat.

8

A FINAL WORD ABOUT NEOCOLONIALISM

Were it not for the tragedy, the irony would seem almost humorous: presidents of the United States send tens of thousands of American youths to their deaths and untold numbers of Asians to theirs ostensibly so that the South Vietnamese will have the privilege of selecting and maintaining their own government, and a leading United States company, ITT, urges the White House to precipitate the downfall of Chile's freely elected president.[1]

The ITT affair has demonstrated with bold clarity a predicament of underdeveloped countries like Chile. On the one hand, they need foreign capital and technology, and on the other, the payment for such necessities is often the loss of their dignity and sovereignty as independent nations. With the expropriation of the Chilean Telephone Company (of which ITT owned 70 percent) in September 1971, ITT quickly presented an 18-point plan to the White House designed to bring about the downfall of the Allende administration. The plan amounted to economic and diplomatic warfare against Chile.

As reported by the *New York Times,* the ITT plan called for a withholding of loans from international agencies. ITT suggested that the White House also "quietly have some large U.S. private banks do the same." Thus one sees how the international loan can be a neocolonial weapon. The plan also called for the United States government to stop purchases of Chilean goods for six months, including copper, the mainstay of Chilean foreign reserves. The White House was urged to "Discuss with the C.I.A. how it can assist in the six-month squeeze." ITT also wanted the

[1] Information about the ITT plan and all quotes are from the *New York Times,* July 3, 1972.

White House to subvert the Chilean armed forces, asking it to "Get to reliable sources within the Chilean military." It wanted a delay in "fuel delivery to navy and gasoline to the air force. . . . United States manufacturers should stop or delay shipments of small arms and ammunition to Chile." The plan also called for steps to "Help disrupt," the United Nations Conference on Trade and Development that was held in Chile in May 1972. Finally, "The United States should consult with other governments whose nationals are suffering from the Chilean Marxists. This would include countries to which Chile owes money."

Chile expropriated ITT's telephone company in late September 1971 and in early October the "war" plan was submitted to the White House. Its purpose was to insure that President Allende did not "get through the crucial next six months." Economic chaos would be created so that the Chilean military would have to step in to restore order.

To its great credit the Nixon administration rejected the ITT plan. On its own account, however, the Nixon administration closed off loans from the Export-Import Bank, the World Bank, and the Inter-American Bank, although it later agreed to a rescheduling of Chile's foreign debt payments.

In addition to rallying support around President Allende, the ITT affair surely must have induced more Chileans to draw the conclusion that the benefits of international capitalism are not always worth the liabilities.

BIBLIOGRAPHY

The purpose of this selected bibliography is to make suggestions for further reading and to indicate some of the more important sources I drew upon in writing this book. Several books not directly related to Chilean history were important to the development of the present book and are highly recommended. On liberalism and the bourgeoisie see Guido de Ruggiero, *The History of European Liberalism* (Boston, 1964). On capitalism see E. J. E. Hobsbawm's introduction to Karl Marx, *Pre-Capitalist Economic Formations* (New York, 1966); Paul M. Sweezy, *The Theory of Capitalist Development* (New York, 1968); Maurice Dobb, *Studies in the Development of Capitalism* (New York, 1968); and Paul A. Baran and Paul M. Sweezy, *Monopoly Capitalism* (New York, 1968). On feudalism see Marc Bloch, *Feudal Society,* 2 vols. (Chicago, 1966); Henri Pirenne, *Medieval Cities* (Princeton, 1969); and E. J. E. Hobsbawm, "A Case of Neo-Feudalism: La Convención, Peru," *Journal of Latin American Studies,* vol. 1, pt. 2 (November 1969). On the transition from capitalism to socialism and liberalism to democracy see E. H. Carr, *The New Society* (New York, 1969) and David Potter, *People of Plenty* (Chicago, 1955).

There were general books on Chilean history that played a vital role in the development of the present work. I have relied on the multivolume works of Diego Barros Arana (*Historia General De Chile,* 2d ed., 12 vols. [Santiago, 1930–1941]) and Francisco Antonio Encina (*Historia De Chile, desde la prehistoria hasta 1891,* 20 vols. [Santiago, 1948–1955]). For those reading Encina a helpful and corrective overview of his massive work is Charles C. Griffin, "Francisco Encina and Revisionism in Chilean History," *Hispanic American Historical Review,* vol. 37, no. 1 (February 1957). See also the very valuable general works by Federico Gil, *The Political System of Chile* (Boston, 1966); Luis Galdames, *A History of Chile* (New York, 1964); Jaime Eyzaguirre, *Fisonomía Histórica de Chile* (Santiago, 1965); Alberto Edwards Vives, *La Fronda Aristocrática,* 5th ed. (Santiago, 1959); and for a leftist interpretation full of interesting thoughts and statistics Julio César Jobet, *Ensayo crítico del desarrollo económico-social de Chile* (Santiago, 1955). See also Daniel Martner's invaluable *Estudio de política comercial chilena e historia económica nacional,* 2 vols. (Santiago, 1923).

In addition to these general works the reader may find Pedro Pablo Figueroa's *Diccionario biográfico general de Chile,* 2d ed. (Santiago, 1889) and Virgilio Figueroa's *Diccionario histórico y biográfico de Chile,* 5 vols. (Santiago, 1925–1931) of considerable use.

Of the many travel accounts that I have read over the years, three were directly useful for the present book. They are Maria Graham, *Journal of a Residence in Chile, During the Year 1822* (London, 1824); Samuel Haigh, *Sketches of Buenos Ayres and Chile* (London, 1829); and John Miers, *Travels in Chile and La Plata,* 2 vols. (London, 1826). Also important was the memoir of a Chilean, Vicente Pérez Rosales's *Recuerdos del pasado* (Santiago, 1943).

For the Spanish background see Jaime Vicens Vives, *An Economic History of Spain* (Princeton, 1969); J. H. Elliot, *Imperial Spain, 1469–1716* (New York, 1966); Richard Herr, *The Eighteenth-Century Revolution in Spain* (Princeton, 1969); and Robert J. Shafer, *The Economic Societies in the Spanish World, 1763–1821* (Syracuse, 1958).

Some of the books mentioned in the following sections deal with more than one period or century in Chilean history. On the colonial period and the two later centuries see Andre Gunder Frank's *Capitalism and Underdevelopment in Latin America: Historical Studies of Chile and Brazil* (New York, 1969). This is a book with many provocative thoughts, one with which I disagree on several fundamental issues. To his great credit, Frank was one of the first to argue that Chile's colonial economy was essentially capitalist and not feudal. Another provocative book is Stanley J. Stein and Barbara H. Stein, *The Colonial Heritage of Latin America* (New York, 1970). On the treatment of the Indians in the colonial period see Eugene H. Korth, S.J., *Spanish Colonial Policy in Colonial Chile* (Stanford, 1968). On the inquilinos see Mario Góngora's excellent *Origin de los "inquilinos" de Chile central* (Santiago, 1960). Slavery is covered in Rolando Mellafe's superb *La Introducción De La Esclavitud Negra En Chile* (Santiago, 1959). Marcello Carmagnani deals with the colonial population in "Colonial Latin American Demography: Growth of Chilean Population, 1700–1830," *Journal of Social History,* vol. 1, no. 2 (Winter 1967), as do Marcello Carmagani and Herbert Klein, "Demografía Histórica: La Población del Obispado de Santiago, 1777–1778," *Boletín de la Academia Chilena de la Historia,* Año 32, no. 72 (Primer Semestre de 1965). I have used Carmagnani's figures in the text. On the Peruvian shipping monopoly see Demetrio Ramos, *Trigo Chileno* (Madrid, 1967); and Sergio Sepúlveda, *El trigo chileno en el mercado mundial* (Santiago, 1956). For commerce I drew heavily on Sergio Villalobos, *El Comercio Y La Crisis Colonial* (Santiago, 1968). See also Ruggiero Romano, *Una economía colonial: Chile en el siglo XVIII* (Buenos Aires, 1965); and Marcello Carmagnani, "La Producción Agropecuaria Chilena: Aspectos Cuantitativos (1680–1830)," *Cahiers Des Amériques Latines,* no. 3 (Janvier–Juin 1969). The collapse of empire and the coming of independence is treated in Luis Vitale, *Interpretación Marxista de la Historia de Chile: La Colonia y la Revolución de 1810* (Santiago, 1968). Vitale also recognizes that the colonial economy was centrally capitalist and not feudal. The same general subject is covered in Hernán Ramírez Necochea, *Antecedentes Económicos de la Independencia de Chile,* 2d. ed. (Santiago, 1967), a Marxist interpretation. Ramírez has been having a running argument with Sergio Villalobos over the causes of independence. Readers of both books will find the argument stimulating. Other works on independence are Inge Wolff, "Algunas Consideraciones Sobre Causas Económicas de la Emancipación Chilena," *Anuario De Estudios Americanos,* vol. 11 (1954); and Jaime Eyzaguirre, *Ideario y ruta de la emancipación Chilena* (Santiago, 1957). The following are excellent studies of the colonial period: Julio Alemparte, *El Cabildo en Chile Colonial,* 2d ed. (Santiago, 1966); Alejandro Fuenzalida Grandón, *La evolución social de Chile (1541–1810)* (Santiago, 1906); María Eugenia Horvitz Vásquez, "Ensayo Sobre El Crédito En Chile Colonial" (unpublished Memoria De Prueba, Santiago, 1966); Elsa L. Urbina Reyes, "El Tribunal Del Consulado En Chile, 1795–1865" (unpublished Memoria De Prueba, Santiago, 1959); José Toribio Medina, *Cosas de la Colonia* (Santiago, 1952); Jacques Barbier, "Elite and Cadres in Bourbon Chile," *Hispanic American Historical Review,* vol. 52, no. 3 (August 1972); Domingo Amunátegui Solar, *Mayorazgos y títulos de castilla,* 3 vols. (Santiago, 1901–1904); and Néstor Meza Villalobos, *La conciencia política chilena durante la Monarquía* (Santiago, 1958).

The independence period is covered in Sergio Villalobos, *Tradición y reforma en 1810* (Santiago, 1961); Miguel Luis Amunátegui Reyes, *La Crónica De 1810,* 2 vols. (Santiago, 1876); and his *Los precursores de la independencia de Chile,* 3 vols. (Santiago, 1910). The following works are excellent on the independence period and early nineteenth century: Julio Alemparte's brilliant *Carrera y Freire* (Santiago, 1963); Simon Collier, *Ideas and Politics of Chilean Independence, 1808–1833* (Cambridge, 1967); Paul Venorden Shaw, *The Early Constitutions of Chile, 1810–1833* (New York, 1930); Marcelo Segall, "Las luchas de las clases en las primeras décadas de la República, 1810–1846," *Anales de la Universidad de Chile,* no. 125 (Primer Trimestre de 1962), a Marxist interpretation; Jaime Eyzaguirre, *O'Higgins,* 3d ed. (Santiago, 1950); Eugenio Orrego Vicuña, *El espíritu constitucional de la administración O'Higgins* (Santiago, 1924) and his *O'Higgins. Vida y Tiempo* (Buenos Aires, 1946); and Francisco Antonio Encina,

Portales, 2 vols. (Santiago, 1934). See also Ramón Sotomayor Valdes's well-regarded *Historia de Chile bajo el gobierno del jeneral D. Joaquín Prieto,* 4 vols. (Santiago, 1900–1903).

A variety of nineteenth-century topics are covered well in the following works: Domingo Amunátegui Solar, *Historia social de Chile* (Santiago, 1932); and the same author's *El progreso intelectual y político de Chile* (Santiago, 1936); Alberto Cruchaga, *Los primeros años del ministerio de relaciones exteriores* (Santiago, 1919); Robert N. Burr, *By Reason or Force: Chile and the Balancing of Power in South America, 1830–1905* (Berkeley, 1967); John J. Johnson, *Pioneer Telegraphy in Chile, 1852–1876* (Stanford, 1948); and Claudio Véliz's extremely valuable *Historia de la marina mercante de Chile* (Santiago, 1961). A broad range of nineteenth- and twentieth-century topics is treated by Frederick B. Pike in *Chile and the United States, 1880–1962* (Notre Dame, 1963). Chilean constitutional history in the nineteenth and twentieth centuries is ably discussed in Luis Galdames, *Historia de Chile: la evolución constitucional* (Santiago, 1925); and Julio Heise González, *150 años de evolución institucional* (Santiago, 1960). Two famous works on political ideas are Ricardo Donoso, *Desarrollo político y social de Chile desde la Constitución de 1833* (Santiago, 1942) and Donoso's *Las ideas políticas en Chile,* 2d ed. (Santiago, 1967). A well-known history of political parties in the past two centuries is Alberto Edwards Vives and Eduardo Frei, *Historia de los partidos políticos chilenos* (Santiago, 1949). The landholding system and agricultural development is discussed in George M. McBride, *Chile: Land and Society* (New York, 1936); and the more up-to-date and valuable work by Arnold J. Bauer, "Chilean Rural Society in the Nineteenth Century" (unpublished doctoral dissertation, The University of California, Berkeley, 1969); and Bauer, "Chilean Rural Labor in the Nineteenth Century," *The American Historical Review,* vol. 76, no. 4 (October 1971). A work of enormous value and influence is Jean Borde and Mario Góngora, *Evolución de la Propiedad Rural en el Valle del Puangue,* 2 vols. (Santiago, 1956). Other interesting studies are Oscar Bermúdez, *Historia del Salitre desde sus orígines hasta la Guerra del Pacífico* (Santiago, 1963); Robert M. Will, "The Introduction of Classical Economics into Chile," *Hispanic American Historical Review,* vol. 44, no. 1 (February 1964); and on the Balmaceda period Harold Blakemore, "The Chilean Revolution of 1891 and Its Historiography," *Hispanic American Historical Review,* vol. 45, no. 3 (August 1965).

For the early twentieth century see Carl Solberg, *Immigration and Nationalism: Argentina and Chile, 1890–1914* (Austin, 1970); and Francisco Antonio Encina, *Nuestra inferioridad económica,* 2d ed. (Santiago, 1955). On the economy see Frank W. Fetter, *Monetary In-*

flation in Chile (Princeton, 1931). Fetter's book has been enormously influential. For a sound criticism see Albert O. Hirschman, *Journeys toward Progress* (New York, 1968). See also Joseph Grunwald, *Desarrollo económico de Chile, 1940–1956* (Santiago, 1956); Ricardo Lagos Escobar, *La concentración del poder económico,* 4th ed. (Santiago, 1962); and Aníbal Pinto Santa Cruz, *Chile, un caso de desarrollo frustrado,* 2d ed. (Santiago, 1962). The preceding three books are of great importance. See also the various essays in Albert O. Hirschman, ed., *Latin American Issues* (New York, 1961), especially the enlightening essay on the "structuralist" school in Chilean development by Grunwald. There are also valuable essays by Aníbal Pinto, Jacques Chonchol, and Osvaldo Sunkel in Claudio Véliz, ed., *Obstacles to Change in Latin America* (New York, 1969). Worthwhile also is Alvin Cohen, *Economic Change in Chile, 1929–1959* (Gainesville, 1960), and P. T. Ellsworth, *Chile: An Economy in Transition* (New York, 1945).

Agriculture and copper are covered in Markos Mamalakis and Clark Winton Reynolds, *Essays on the Chilean Economy* (New Haven, 1965), which I followed closely. On copper see Mario Vera Valenzuela, *La política económica del Cobre en Chile* (Santiago, 1961). Ernest Feder, "Feudalism and Agricultural Development: The Role of Controlled Credit in Chile's Agriculture," *Land Economics,* vol. 36, no. 1 (February 1960) is important on agricultural credit. Of importance is Gene Ellis Martin, *La División de la tierra en Chile central* (Santiago, 1960). I followed Martin's work closely for my agricultural sections. See also Marvin J. Sternberg's valuable "Chilean Land Tenure and Land Reform" (unpublished doctoral dissertation, The University of California, Berkeley, 1962). Many recent researchers have emphasized the interconnections between large landowners and industry and business. Sternberg has found some large landowners who have invested only in agriculture. A fine study is William C. Thiesenhusen, *Chile's Experiments in Agrarian Reform* (Madison, 1966).

For many topics see James Petras, *Politics and Social Forces in Chilean Development* (Berkeley, 1970), which is loaded with data and valuable insights. See also the North American Congress on Latin America's *New Chile* (New York, 1972), which also contains a wide variety of data. Both are contributions from the left. Also for many topics see Kalman H. Silvert's *American Universities Field Staff Newsletter* of October 20, 1956; November 22 and 25, 1956; January 1 and 27, 1957; April 11, 1957; and August 30, 1957.

The classic work on the Popular Front is John Reese Stevenson, *The Chilean Popular Front* (Philadelphia, 1942). A forceful account of the Alessandri era is Ricardo Donoso, *Alessandri: Agitador y demoledor: Cincuenta años de historia política de Chile,* 2 vols. (Mexico City,

1952–1954). An important recent book on the military is Frederick Nunn, *Chilean Politics, 1920–1931: The Honorable Mission of the Armed Forces* (Albuquerque, 1970). Ibáñez is discussed in Donald W. Bray, "Chilean Politics during the Second Ibáñez Government, 1952–58," (unpublished doctoral dissertation, Stanford University, 1961). On education see Eduardo Hamuy, *Educación elemental, analfabetismo y desarrollo económico* (Santiago, 1960). Many topics are covered in Ernst Halperin, *Nationalism and Communism in Chile* (Cambridge, Mass., 1965); Ben G. Burnett, *Political Groups in Chile: The Dialogue between Order and Change* (Austin, 1970); and Mario Zañartu and John J. Kennedy, eds., *The Overall Development of Chile* (Notre Dame, 1969).

I relied on my own works heavily and followed some of them very closely in writing the present book. They are: *Diego Portales: Interpretative Essays on the Man and Times* (The Hague, 1967); *Bernardo O'Higgins* (New York, 1968); *The Spanish American Independence Movement* (Chicago, 1973); "The Business Activities of William Wheelwright in Chile, 1829–1860" (unpublished doctoral dissertation, New York University, 1964); "The Political Influence of the British Merchants Resident in Chile during the O'Higgins Administration, 1817–1823," *The Americas,* vol. 27, no. 1 (July 1970); and "The Political Status of the Chilean Merchants at Independence: The Concepción Example, 1790–1810," *The Americas,* vol. 29, no. 1 (July 1972).

INDEX